# OUTBOUND

A Pragmatic Guide to
International Business

MATHEW SEGAL

Copyright © 2021 by Mathew Segal. All rights reserved.

The information provided within this Book is for general informational purposes only. Even though we have attempted to present accurate information, there are no representations or warranties, express or implied, about the completeness, accuracy, or reliability of the information, products, services, or related graphics contained in this Book for any purpose. The information is provided "as is," to be used at your own risk.

No part of this book may be reproduced or transmitted in any form or by any means, electronic or mechanical, without written permission from the author.

All trademarks appearing in this Book are the property of their respective owners.

No warranty may be created or extended by any promotional statements for this work. The author shall not be liable for any damages arising herefrom.

ISBN 978-1-7375182-0-4

Cover Design: Najdan Mancic
Book Design: Najdan Mancic

TABLE OF CONTENTS

Introduction ..................................................................5

**SECTION ONE: Setting the Stage** ........................**11**
   **Chapter One:** Look Before You Leap ....................13
   **Chapter Two:** Planning for Growth .......................21

**SECTION TWO: Where**............................................**31**
   **Chapter Three:** Close to Home................................33
   **Chapter Four:** A Framework for Assessing New Markets ....41
   **Chapter Five:** Using Competitive Data ..................54
   **Chapter Six:** FDI/Investing.......................................62
   **Chapter Seven:** Trade Agreements ..........................67

**SECTION THREE: How** ............................................**77**
   **Chapter Eight:** Business Models ..............................79
   **Chapter Nine:** Finding New Customers.................85
   **Chapter Ten:** Pricing...................................................93
   **Chapter Eleven:** Shipping and Collecting...................106
   **Chapter Twelve:** Working with Distributors...............118
   **Chapter Thirteen:** Managing Risk ...........................130
   **Chapter Fourteen:** International Growth Drivers ......147

Appendix A: Checklist of Key Requirements .....................158
Appendix B: Summary of Helpful Planning Resources ........162

INTRODUCTION

I'm writing the book I wish I had access to over the past 25 years: while in business school to bring context to the academic discussions in the classroom; before entering the management consulting world and advising clients on how to grow their businesses; and before joining a client to develop and implement a global growth strategy.

Yes, it would have been helpful then, but here we are. Now, with 25 years of advisory and management experience behind me, I'm codifying my learnings on international business into a pragmatic guide that will hopefully spare you much of the pain and mistakes I've encountered along the way. While I cover a few strategic frameworks to support structured decision-making, my objective here is not to present some earth-shattering new academic paradigm.

What we will do is explore—in a real-world manner—some key strategic and practical issues that management teams need to grapple with in international expansion, and present some practical guidance on how to address them to increase their odds of success. Regardless of the vantage point from which you're reading this book, my goal is that you come away with 10 or so tangible, practical ideas on how to better manage international growth for your business, portfolio companies, or clients.

## WHO IS THIS BOOK FOR?

- ► Senior management teams / executives initiating or prioritizing international growth efforts
- ► Sales and business development leaders looking for growth opportunities in international markets
- ► Consultants advising clients on issues related to international expansion and globalization
- ► Private equity / VC investors pursing targets with international growth opportunity, or serving as a board advisor to portfolio companies
- ► Professional service providers who are looking to expand beyond their area of subject matter expertise
- ► Lawyers seeking to understand key non-legal drivers in international expansion
- ► Students studying business at the undergraduate or graduate levels
- ► Anyone else interested in a pragmatic view of globalization

## MY BACKGROUND

I want to share a bit about me so you understand my perspective. I've spent a lot of time and made a lot of mistakes from which I've learned valuable lessons in international markets. The first chapter of my 20+ year post-MBA career was largely theoretical—as a management consultant working with global clients on a range of business challenges in various sectors. Great experience, but largely academic; our job was typically done after the final presentation was delivered. It was up to the management teams to execute.

The ensuing chapter swung to the other side of the professional spectrum, as head of the international business for a US-based, private equity-owned battery manufacturer (one of my ex-clients)—truly the epitome of "getting your hands dirty." In that role, I led a dispersed global team that managed a network of distributors, OEMs, and other commercial partners in over 80 countries. Our goal was to transform the company from one that sold some product internationally to a true global enterprise. It was a long journey, with lot of bumps in the road, but we made a lot of good progress. I also learned a ton about the practical realities of international business along the way.

I'm now back in an advisory role, applying lessons learned from both chapters, to help companies develop and implement pragmatic plans to expand abroad, optimize their existing businesses overseas, or in some cases, unwind existing efforts to re-focus on more strategic or profitable activities here at home.

## HOW THIS BOOK IS ORGANIZED

There's no way a single book can cover all topics related to international business in a thoughtful and comprehensive manner, and I don't attempt to do that here. Instead, the content of the book mostly addresses two critical high-level framing questions:

- *Where* to go?
- *How* to get there?

The supporting chapters that help answer these fundamental questions are relatively short but should inform your thinking on the topic, provide a helpful resource or two, and most importantly, flag issues that you'll likely need to address in your own business journey. Even if a particular chapter is not directly relevant to your role or interest, I would suggest skimming for key questions/issues. The chapters are relatively short and together provide a roadmap to help you succeed overseas. There's no glossary in this book—if you stumble over a term or some jargon, Google it.

## A FINAL THOUGHT OR TWO

This book was written from my individual perspective. Yours will certainly be different and I'm always interested in learning from other people's experience. I'm also happy to answer questions or expand on a particular point or topic if needed—just send any comments or questions you might have to msegal@terrafirmastrategy.com. It is also written from the point of view of US companies exporting abroad. That said, if you are based in another country, much of the concepts, content, and resources here should still apply.

Finally, I invite you to visit my website www.terrafirmastrategy.com. There's nothing for sale, but there are a fair number of resources and tools that can be helpful as you plan for and execute your plans for international growth.

SECTION ONE
# SETTING THE STAGE

*Marcus Aurelius has a great quote about obstacles to progress: "The impediment to action advances action. What stands in the way becomes the way." In other words, the key to progress is turning challenges on their head, learning from them, and finding a better course forward. This is the mindset required to succeed in the international marketplace: flexibility, creativity, resilience, and dedication. The rewards can be huge, but they will not come easily. So before jumping in, let's set the stage with a dose of reality.*

CHAPTER ONE

# Look Before You Leap

I'm not going to spend a lot of time discussing the importance of international trade or arguing that businesses should look abroad for new markets or operational support. The numbers themselves make the case; in 2019 alone, US exports of manufactured goods totaled close to $2T. Global foreign direct investment (which we'll discuss later) added another $1.4T in international economic activity. It won't be a straight line, but there's no turning back. We're in a global economy.

Regardless of your particular rationale, the business case for expanding abroad can be compelling. On paper, or in a conference room, it can be relatively easy to outline a strategy that can quickly drop EBITDA to the bottom line or open up massive markets not available domestically.

As we all know, however, business is hard—even in well-known, established markets. Winning on the international front is that much harder. Every challenge you face domestically is magnified when you cross the border. Pricing challenges in the US? Try pricing in India and China. Logistical issues getting product from East Coast to West? Nothing compared to shipping containers to the African continent.

With that context, there are key considerations to keep in mind as you embark on, plan for, or optimize your own journey abroad. These are not meant to dissuade, but rather to paint a realistic picture of what's involved so you can enter clear-eyed and plan accordingly (many of these issues will be covered in detail in later chapters).

## KEY CONSIDERATIONS WHEN 'GOING GLOBAL'

1. **Cost:** International expansion is expensive. Companies often overlook—or underestimate—many of the direct costs of globalization, not to mention the hard-to-identify-and-quantify indirect costs. Every company naturally has a unique set of cost dynamics, but there are some general buckets to keep in mind as you assess your own business:

    ### Direct Costs

    ▶ **Headcount**—Simply adding additional tasks to already overloaded, domestically-focused staff is a recipe for failure; it is critical to invest in resources with international business experience in key functional roles, many of which will be incremental to current resource levels.

- **Legal**—Every new country entered will require some level of investment in legal activities; for example, adjustments to standard distribution agreements, IP protection, legal entity analysis and formation, and country-specific employment agreements. These fees can pile up very quickly.

- **Cost of Capital**—Unseating incumbents in new markets often requires offering more aggressive terms than those offered in your home market. It's important to understand the real cost of, say, moving to Net90 from Net30 in new markets, and how that will scale with growth in overseas volume.

- **Capital Expenditures**—Success in new markets often requires modifications to localize your offering. Even if minor, what new equipment might be required to make needed product modifications in new markets? Similarly, what is the cost of carrying specialized inventory for new markets?

- **Travel**—Transitioning to a true global company requires that team members from the CEO down spend time in the field with employees, customers, suppliers, partners, etc. International travel is expensive, but often gets buried in general T&E.

## Indirect Costs

- **Opportunity**—Every minute spent on a plane to China, in a meeting discussing product requirements for Brazil, or with lawyers reviewing privacy requirements in the

EU, is a minute not spent on growing your core business domestically. It may be hard to quantify, but there is potentially a real cost in terms of lost domestic business that absolutely needs to be considered.

- ▶ **Lost Efficiency**—Line changeovers, process adjustments, policy modifications . . .there are an unexpectedly high number of minor operational and procedural adjustments that ripple through organizations as they grow internationally. In the aggregate, these disruptions can compound into a material loss of efficiency for your company.

- ▶ **Management Time**—The executive team, across every function, needs to be fully committed to globalizing the company. This cannot be just one more "strategic initiative" that is added to monthly steering committee meetings. What will be taken off the list to make room? And what is the cost in terms of lost revenue or increased risk of doing so?

2. **Risk:** Doing business internationally increases an organization's risk across several dimensions. Much of this risk can be mitigated with good planning, competent lawyers, and thoughtful execution. If your company's not in the position to dedicate the time, money, or resources here, however, the risk could potentially more than offset the upside of success in new geographies. Risk management is an industry unto its own, but here are a few illustrative risks to consider as you weigh costs/benefits of growing your business abroad:

- ▶ **FCPA/Compliance**—Every company, of any size, doing business internationally needs a formalized compliance and risk management regime. More on this later, but the potential downside of an FCPA or UK Bribery Act violation is just way too high to ignore.

- ▶ **Bad Debt**—As mentioned above, growing into new markets usually requires taking a more aggressive approach to trade terms. Some companies can grow in a real way by selling products cash in advance or under letter of credit, but most need to offer terms to drive customer conversion. Again, much can be done process-wise to minimize bad debt, but offering credit in foreign markets, particularly developing ones, will undoubtedly necessitate an increase in bad debt reserves.

- ▶ **Currency/FX**—Are you selling in US dollars or local currency? Are overseas employees paid in local currency? Are you holding assets overseas? Even small businesses with a limited footprint outside the country can be significantly impacted by fluctuations in exchange rates. A strengthening dollar, for example, can quickly wipe out profits of sales commenced in local currency.

- ▶ **Brand**—A major misstep in the march toward globalization can have a lasting impact on your brand. With social media's insatiable appetite for the next viral meme, the risk here is greater than ever. The American Dairy Association, for instance, replicated its "Got Milk?" campaign in Spanish-speaking countries, where the slogan was translated into "Are You Lactating?" Don't make the same mistake.

- **Distribution**—In their rush to grow sales overseas, companies often take an extremely US-centric view on how they do business with distributors (and other partners). For example, penalties for improper termination of distribution agreements can vary significantly from country to country. To illustrate, in Belgium a distributor can seek lost profits (goodwill indemnity) as well as a range of other costs and compensation if terminated in violation of local laws/procedures, whereas Mexican law does not provide specific indemnification rights for the distributor even if termination is not based on just cause.

3. **Complexity:** International business is complex. There are literally hundreds of drivers/touchpoints/processes that must be localized or augmented to be successful abroad. Questions like:

    - "What adjustments do we need to make to our customer service hours to address issues in Japan?"
    - "Do we have anyone in the group that speaks Japanese?"
    - "What marketing material needs to be translated into Japanese?"
    - "How will we handle warranty claims?"
    - "Do we need a Japanese-language website, and if so, what key words do we need to buy to drive traffic to the site, and on what platforms?"

    While extensive and wide ranging, none of these issues are impossible to address. The key point is that the additional levels of complexity stemming from international business dynamics require thoughtful planning and a bias for action to be addressed in an effective and efficient manner. If your organization is not in a position to tackle this challenge at this point in time, you may be better off waiting.

4. **Time:** From finding and vetting distributors to getting products in the hands of new customers (and everything in between), standard business practices typically take significantly more time and effort to execute overseas, as does realizing the ultimate financial benefits of international growth. An analysis of 20,000 companies in 30 countries by the *Harvard Business Review*, for example, found that companies selling abroad had an average Return on Assets (ROA) of negative one percent as long as five years after their move.

What is your time horizon? Is yours a private equity owned business with a three-year window before the next transaction? Or is it a public company that needs to manage expectations around the quarterly financial impact of international market activities? Are you a closely held family business that has the luxury of taking the long view on major strategic initiatives? Whatever your situation, expect that things will take much longer than assumed. My recommendation here is to plan conservatively by **doubling the time** and **halving the expected return** on new international business.

In the end, many companies never get beyond a toe in the water when it comes to globalizing. They may have a distributor or two overseas, but the bulk of their business is, and will remain, domestic. The reason is usually that despite the allure of big new markets, international business is tough—it's expensive to do right, risky (even on a small scale), and extremely complex relative to the familiar territory of domestic markets. And, on top of all that, even if done "right," real financial benefits can sit far off into the future. The opportunities are out there, no doubt, but you need to start with managed expectations. A thoughtful, data driven strategy; deep executional planning; and the resources, management, and shareholder commitment to tackle unforeseen challenges are required to see these plans through.

CHAPTER TWO

# Planning for Growth

## THE IMPORTANCE OF GOOD PLANNING

Given the challenges discussed, any meaningful effort to expand internationally should include some heavy lifting upfront from a planning perspective. While the concept is straightforward—understanding what needs to be in place across various functions to succeed internationally—even some of the largest and best-known companies in the world can get it wrong. For example:

- **The Home Depot, China**—In 2006, Home Depot bought the Chinese home improvement company Home Way and its 12 stores in the country. Unfortunately, only later did the leading US retailer discover that DIY trends in the Western world didn't translate to the Chinese market. Unlike in much of the west, where DIY home improvement is a hobby for weekend warriors, developing countries in general tend to see DIY as a sign of poverty. By 2012, Home Depot shuttered its stores in China and took a $160M after-tax hit for its troubles.

- **Walmart, Germany**—Walmart has successfully entered dozens of international markets, but Germany isn't one of them. In 1997, Walmart bought two local chains to enter the German market with a total of 85 stores. Ten years later, Walmart abandoned the largest retail market in Europe for good after losing an estimated $1B in the process. A variety of strategic and cultural factors contributed to this failure including pricing (Walmart was forced to raise prices after being charged with predatory pricing), poor employee relations, and "friendly" US customer practices that ended up alienating German shoppers (for example, the greeter at the door was considered creepy).

- **eBay, Japan**—To date, eBay has successfully entered 180 markets globally. In Japan, however, eBay never got traction and shut down in 2002, only two years after entering the world's third largest economy. Why was eBay successful in dozens of other markets but not Japan? Timing was one big issue; eBay entered the market about six months after Yahoo! More importantly, Yahoo! waited until it had established a local brand—and the trust of Japanese consumers—before implementing a transaction fee. On the other hand, eBay implemented standard transaction fees from day one, which was a major deterrent to user adoption, particularly since Japan was largely a cash-based economy at the time. Volume lagged, and eBay was never able to drive enough transactions to reach critical mass.

The point here is that even large, sophisticated companies can fail to ask and answer key planning questions when going abroad. The Home Depot basically got the question of *Where?* wrong—its foundational business model built on DIY enthusiasts simply didn't find a receptive market in China, despite the sheer size of the consumer class. On the other hand, eBay made a major tactical mistake. Had it focused on building a brand and volume before implementing its traditional transaction fee, the outcome may have been vastly different. Walmart seems to have missed the boat on several key questions in Germany. Structural limitations on pricing prevented the retailer from realizing its lowest-price market positioning, while failure to localize its employee and customer practices eroded any remaining chance for success.

## SIMPLIFYING THE PLANNING PROCESS

At the end of the day there are five basic, yet critical, questions you'll need to address when expanding abroad: *Why? When? What? How?* and *Where?* Seems simple, but if you don't have a good answer for these questions—backed by solid analysis, firsthand market input, and a pragmatic approach—you're setting yourself up for failure. As mentioned in the introduction, I chose to focus this book on the *Where?* and the *How?* These tend to be broader questions that lend themselves to general frameworks relevant to just about any organization.

The first three, on the other hand, tend to be a bit narrower in scope and will be highly specific to your particular organization. We'll cover them briefly here to trigger some thinking but won't go into too much detail beyond that.

## WHY?

This seems like a silly question, but a critical first step is defining exactly *why* you want to expand internationally, and ensuring the management team is on board with the rationale and supporting objectives. For example, from a financial perspective:

- Is your primary objective revenue/unit growth?
- Is your business under pressure to bring unit production costs down by fully utilizing that brand new $50M production line?
- Or, on the other hand, is your primary objective to increase margins under increasingly constrained production capacity?
- Are you willing to replace some low margin domestic business with what you hope to be more profitable sales in international markets?
- Is this a defensive move to head off a competitor that's quickly gaining share in international markets, also threatening your share domestically?
- Are you being pulled into international markets by your domestic OEMs who themselves are expanding overseas? Do they require just-in-time supply in China like they

now enjoy in the US? Do they need product to supply their dealers through aftermarket parts and services in countries on three different continents?

And of course, it may not just be about revenue growth or improved profitability. There are a range of other reasons that could potentially justify a merger, acquisition, or greenfield investment abroad. Let's take the case of (fictional) US-based Acme Toothpick Company ("AT"). There are lots of reasons AT might expand abroad, for example:

1. **Lower production costs (labor, regulatory, etc.)**—AT sets up a plant in Vietnam where production costs are half that of Texas.

2. **Access to natural resources**—AT buys timber land in Canada for a steady source of raw materials.

3. **Market proximity**—AT sets up a distribution center in Peru to serve Central and South American distributors who require just-in-time shipments.

4. **Export platform**—AT sets up a plant in Malaysia, not to reduce production costs, but rather to sell into the ASEAN Trade markets tariff-free, thus avoiding a 20% adder to landed cost.

5. **Revenue growth**—AT sets up a sales and service office in Russia to better compete with local competitors. By doing so, AT is perceived as being a committed local supplier.

6. **Tariff-jumping**—AT sets up a small plant in India to avoid massive tariffs on imported toothpicks.

7. **Logistical optimization**—AT sets up a packaging operation in Turkey where it can more cost effectively package private label toothpicks for distribution in the EU.
8. **Financial incentives**—AT sets up an entity in Ireland where it can run its EU operation at a lower corporate tax rate.
9. **Access to capabilities**—AT buys a company in Romania that has needed plastic molding toothpick engineering capabilities.

Whatever the rationale, having a clear view of your strategic objectives, corresponding key milestones, and tangible metrics for success will provide essential context for your international growth strategy going forward.

## WHEN?

Meeting any of the objectives defined above will take time, money, focus, and managerial perseverance. Even with a bulletproof strategy, ripe market conditions, and an enthusiastic team of managers, taking the plunge at the wrong time can be a critical mistake. What that right time is will be unique to your particular circumstances, but there are several key factors that should be considered:

1. **Business cycles**—Are you better off launching your international growth strategy during a down cycle domestically, to allow for greater focus? What about the target country(ies)? Will you be more successful easing in, or jumping into a cycle of high local growth/demand?

2. **Other priorities**—If your business is like most others, there are already too many strategic initiatives facing the senior management team as it is. Will development and implementation of an international growth strategy be just one more on the steering committee's bowler chart, or is the timing right to give it the focus and attention it needs in light of competing priorities? Again, assume things will take twice as long and yield half the results before finalizing that commitment.

3. **Investment Cycles**—Are your shareholders looking for an exit in the next couple years or are they in it for long-term value creation? If the horizon is less than two or three years and you're starting from scratch, it is unlikely that any substantial EBITDA will be generated to drive shareholder value in a transaction. If, on the other hand, international growth is a key investment thesis of a potential buyer, having established some traction in terms of real sales in high growth international markets should be reflected in increased transaction multiples, likely providing a healthy return on time and investment ahead of a potential sale.

A quick example on the issue of timing: one of my recent clients, a $1B+ public company in the business services space, made a knee-jerk reaction to grow internationally via acquisition about eight years prior to my involvement. I was brought in to help optimize their international footprint, which had been just about breakeven since the very beginning. It became very clear early on that the right thing to do would be to sell it off completely and focus exclusively on the domestic market where the client had a competitive advantage, significant room for growth, and much better margins. At some point, perhaps it would have made sense to grow abroad, but they simply made the jump too soon.

## WHAT?

What are you selling in international markets and how does that differ by region and country? Even some of the largest, most respected names in business fail to appropriately localize their offering to their target market. A good example is Apple, which we all think of as fully embodying thoughtful, targeted strategy and product development. Well, that wasn't always the case. When Apple launched its flagship product, the Apple II in Europe in the early '80s, it did so with an American keyboard that failed to provide many standard characters needed in Europe, including umlauts, accents, and other special punctuation. The result was a largely unusable machine that was pulled from the market in 1983. The topic of product localization is a discipline unto itself, but a few key principles can help guide your thinking:

- ▶ **Prioritize**—Lead with specific products / services that will establish a foothold with the least amount of complexity necessary.

- ▶ **Localize regionally**—Determine whether modifications being made for entry into one market also meet local requirements in other, adjacent geographies. This can help scale growth down the road.

- **Don't over-localize**—Making major product modifications for each new country will be hard to scale and add unneeded complexity to the business. Do the minimum required to meet local requirements.

- **Conform**—Ensure your offering meets local standards for safety, labeling, and other regulatory requirements

- **Do no harm**—Check that your naming, logo, and general branding conveys the intended message in the local market; or at a minimum, that it does not offend your target audience.

In the end, having clearly defined objectives for expanding abroad (why?), doing so at the right time (when?), and going to market with the right product or service (what?) are all essential for the success of your international business. But, as mentioned, these will be highly unique to your particular business and a bit more discreet in their answers: The time is now; our goal is 20% revenue growth over three years; let's lead with our B2C offering.

Decisions on **where** to go and **how** best to succeed, on the other hand, tend to be broader in scope and involve many more shades of gray in defining the best path forward. My goal for the remainder of the book, therefore, is to provide frameworks, resources, lessons learned, and perspectives to get as close to the "right" answer as possible.

SECTION TWO
# WHERE

*Rarely is the question of **where** to focus addressed in a vacuum. If you're running an existing business, you may already be exporting into a handful of countries and deciding where to plant a flag for increased focus and investment. If you're conducting due diligence on a potential acquisition with international growth as upside opportunity, you may be assessing an existing business plan with markets and associated revenue already identified and quantified. If you're building a plant overseas, the question may be where to leverage a physical presence into increased commercial opportunity as well.*

*The hypotheticals are numerous; however, taking a methodical, yet pragmatic, approach to answering the **where?** question is a critical step. The ensuing pages are not meant to answer the question specifically, but rather outline some helpful frameworks, posit key questions, and provide helpful resources that you can tweak and apply to your own journey to make the ride a little smoother.*

CHAPTER THREE

# Close to Home

There's a natural inclination to be allured by the potential of large, quickly growing foreign markets. While COVID has certainly shaken things up, non-stop headlines like, "India's Consumer Spending Set to Boom!" and, "BRICS to Play a Leading Role in Driving Future Global Economic Growth!" have been front and center in business reporting over the past decade or so. These reports get desired clicks as they speak to our inherent drive to find the pot of gold at the end of the rainbow . . . but what does the data really tell us about the current state and trendline for various export markets?

Let's move beyond the headlines, cut and dice actual merchandise export data to see if the reality matches the hype, and determine what the implications might be for your business.

While this is taken from the US perspective, many of the key themes will apply to other large global exporters as well.

## EXPORT MARKET SIZE

The most basic indicator we can look at to compare destinations is simply market size; i.e., in dollar terms, how much, as a nation, are we actually exporting to various countries around the world? Given the sensationalist nature of business news, the actual data may not match your pre-conceived assumptions on export concentration. *(Note: we use 2019 data here since it was the last full year pre-COVID)*

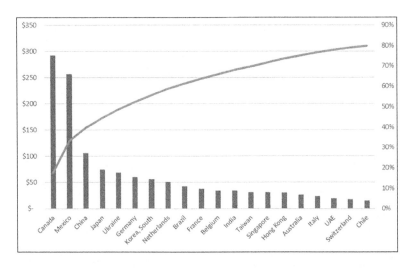

**Chart:** *Top 20 countries for US Merchandise Exports, 2019 ($Bs and % of total)*

## Key Observations:

1. **Very high levels of export concentration:**

   ▶ In the aggregate, US companies exported goods to 233 countries in 2019, ranging from $292.6B (Canada) to $6.2M (Pitcairn Islands). Despite the breadth of US exports, actual $ value is concentrated in relatively few countries.

- Canada and Mexico alone represent over one-third of all US exports. This is not surprising given free trade, proximity, history, etc., but still represents a huge piece of the total export market.
- Adding in China and Japan, export concentration jumps to 48% among the top 4 countries (out of 233 total!).
- Less than 10% of the total number of countries account for over 80% of all merchandise exports—the 80/20 rule is conservative when it comes to US exports.
- 20% of export markets (46 countries) represent ~95% of total exports. Put differently, the bottom 80% of countries account for only 5% of total exports.

2. **Developing markets:**

- Despite all the hype around growing consumer classes in India, it ranked 12th in 2019 in US merchandise exports, behind much smaller countries like Belgium, Ukraine, and the Netherlands.
- The BRICI countries (Brazil, Russia, India, China, and Indonesia) represent a large chunk of trade ($197.1B) in the aggregate, but over two-thirds of that went to China. Brazil, Russia, India, and Indonesia combined accounted for $90.7B, less than one-third of Canada's total in 2019.

## Strategic questions for your business:

- Are we overlooking key, export friendly markets (i.e., Mexico and Canada) to chase low probability opportunities in trendier locations?

▶ Is there something unique about our business (product, footprint, channel, etc.) that will enable success in large, but ostensibly difficult to penetrate markets like India or Brazil? Likewise, are we fully aware of the operational, commercial, and/or structural factors that make these markets difficult to penetrate, and if so, how do we have a plan to overcome these hurdles?

## MARKET GROWTH: 5-YEAR COMPOUND ANNUAL GROWTH RATE (CAGR), 2014-2019

When factoring in annual growth in exports over the recent past, a more nuanced picture emerges in terms of relative market attractiveness for US exports:

**Chart:** *Market size vs. 5-year CAGR for top 20 counties for US Merchandise Exports, 2019 (Mexico, Canada, and China excluded)*

## Key Observations:

- I've removed Mexico (1.3% CAGR), Canada (-1.3% CAGR), and China (-3.0% CAGR) given they're outliers from a volume standpoint, but it's important to note that from a growth standpoint, the three largest US markets have essentially been stagnant over the past five years.

- Despite being relatively small in total exports, India has seen strong growth in export volume (which actually fits with the media narrative in recent years). At close to 10%, it's the highest of any country in the top 50 aside from Vietnam at 13.6% and Poland at 10.2%.

- How important are growth rates at the macro level? Assuming (not realistically of course) that growth rates continue unchanged for the next 10 years, India's export volume will increase significantly, but only to ~$60B, still just one-fifth the export size of Mexico and one-sixth of Canada.

## Strategic questions for your business:

- Is our strategy focused on taking share of an already established export market or are we trying to get in early on a fast growing vertical in a developing country?

- Have we established a foothold in smaller, "under the radar" markets that will enable us to capitalize on strong demand for US products over time?

- Are we tracking key drivers (e.g., trade deals, politics, exchange rates) that may impact strength of demand for US products in these markets going forward, and if so, are we planning accordingly as it relates to our business?

## US EXPORTS PER CAPITA

A third cut that provides some insight into relative market attractiveness for US exporters is overall export value *per capita* in key markets. The below chart is derived by simply dividing total export value by the destination country's current population.

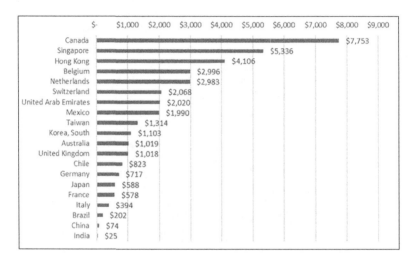

**Chart:** *Per Capita Value of by country for top 20 counties for US Merchandise exports, 2019 ($USD)*

## Key Observations:

▶ Given differences in population and relative wealth, we would expect significant differences in the per capita "value" of key export destinations. That said, the gaps here are massive. A few highlights:

▷ Each "consumer" in Canada is worth nearly 400 times that of each consumer in India

- ▷ Exports to Mexico are more than three times that of Japan on a per capita basis, despite the fact that Japan has the world's third largest economy with GDP more than four times that of Mexico

- ▶ Even within certain regions, significant differences exist in relative per capita value, e.g.,

  - ▷ Belgium is over seven times that of Italy
  - ▷ France, which is largely considered a key destination for US goods, consumes only 20% of the export volume of the Netherlands, a sister EU country, on a per capita basis

- ▶ When comparing China to India (as people often do), it's clear from this cut at least that China represents significantly more value than India on a per capita basis (three times as much). That said, both are still just a fraction of many non-BRICI countries.

## Strategic questions for your business:

- ▶ Can we get high enough penetration/conversion in larger, developing markets like India to make up for the lower value per customer relative to more established export markets?

- ▶ Do we need wide adoption to justify entering an export market, or is our target market small, identifiable, and reachable?

- Do we have a country/market-specific plan for the Euro Zone or are we treating the region as a single market in terms of customer demand?

- Where can we get the biggest bang for our buck in terms of time and energy spent on customer conversion?

## CONCLUSION

There are a host of obvious reasons Canada and Mexico are far and away the US' largest export markets. They're close, relatively easy to do business in, have favorable trade deals, common history, shared cultures . . . the list goes on. There are an equally large number of reasons why India, despite the sheer size of its population and growing consumer class, still consumes a relatively small percentage of US merchandise exports: high duties, price competition, channel complexity and distance are just a few (among dozens in my experience!).

Macro export data, while not perfect, provides some good directional insight into how these myriad factors translate into actual dollars spent on US goods. The data shows it's a fairly efficient market out there. And while each business is unique, export trends can and should help guide strategic and tactical plans for expanding into international markets, including maximizing low hanging fruit (e.g., Canada and Mexico), avoiding spinning wheels in potentially very challenging markets (e.g., India and Brazil), and focusing for longer term, strategic bets going forward (e.g., Vietnam, Poland).

CHAPTER FOUR

# A Framework for Assessing New Markets

Determining which countries/geographies on which to focus is obviously a critical question to the ultimate success of your globalization efforts. Unfortunately, there is no simple answer, bullet-proof model, or surefire algorithm here to give you needed answers. Prioritizing markets will require a combination of thoughtful frameworks, heavy analytical lifting, common sense, existing market knowledge, and intuition.

It's helpful to consider a few high-level themes before either engaging outside consultants to do the heavy lifting or embarking on your strategic journey alone:

1. **Focus**—Narrowing your target list down to a manageable number of countries/geographies can be difficult, particularly if you're in the earlier stages of international growth. That

said, I strongly recommend focusing your efforts on fewer rather than more target geographies. The world is a big place, and the inclination here may be to take a shotgun approach and see what sticks. But unless luck is on your side, diluting your efforts will likely result in a lot of wasted time, energy, money and lost motivation.

After taking some of the key steps described in this book, put a stake in the ground and go. Even if it ends up being a sub-optimal geography, getting some wins on the board early will provide needed learnings and momentum to live to fight another day (in perhaps a more attractive end market). The same holds true if your business is a little more mature, and you're already selling into a number of countries. Align your development efforts with where you expect the bulk of profitable growth to come from going forward, resisting the temptation to chase opportunities that might derail focused efforts.

2. **Understand the Impact on the Organization**—If you're already selling internationally, you know that every function within your business will be impacted by further expansion abroad. Executive buy-in and support is only step one. HR will have to learn how to hire and manage employees (or contractors) in foreign markets with a whole different set of rules, regulations, and cultural norms; finance will have to manage credit terms and risk in potentially dozens of economies; marketing will have to translate collateral into different languages and adjust messaging to address local market tastes and communication styles. Ensure that functional leaders have the capabilities and resources required

to enter foreign markets and/or support expected growth in business and complexity over time. The organization will only be as strong as the weakest link as it relates to international business capabilities.

3. **Plan Conservatively**—Strategic plans, in just about any business setting, are notoriously optimistic when it comes to financial upside, cost and timeframes. This dynamic is amplified dramatically when dealing in international markets for obvious reasons—distance, culture, language, and logistics all come into play, to name just a few.

   As alluded to earlier, a good rule of thumb here is what I've come to call the "Rule of 2s." It's pretty simple. At a minimum, double both the time and the cost it will take to take the reach a forecast contribution number. So, if a business plan you're reviewing estimates revenue in three years will be $100M, with $10M (10%) in EBITDA. Assume it will take six years to hit the topline number with only half the expected contribution. So, three years out you can expect revenues of more like $50M with $2.5M in EBITDA contribution (5% not 10%). This may feel like a conservative approach but almost all the unknowns in entering a new market—even with good planning—will slow you down or require more time and money to overcome. Rarely does it work the other way around.

4. **Don't Chase the Shiny Object**—As discussed, large and growing consumer classes in developing countries can be enticing, but don't fall into the market share trap—"if we only get 1% share in this massive market, it will be a game

changer for us." Particularly if your business is relatively new to international markets, getting your feet wet in a more traditional, familiar market (e.g., Canada, or the UK) can help your organization move along the learning curve as you plan for higher risk, higher reward initiatives down the road.

## CAN WE/SHOULD WE?—A FRAMEWORK FOR PRIORITIZING EXPANSION EFFORTS

Fundamentally, how to prioritize expansion efforts abroad boils down to two key questions:

1. *Should We?* focus on the market in question—essentially, how attractive is the market strategically relative to other options for international expansion?
2. *Can We?* penetrate into the market in question—regardless of how attractive the market is, are we in a position to execute on the tactical requirements necessary to successfully enter the market?

People tend to get in the weeds on the *Should We?* and gloss over the *Can We?*. "We'll figure it out once we get there" is a common, but dangerous, approach. I would argue that whether or not you have the capability to enter a market is actually much more important than its strategic attractiveness (once a minimum threshold is reached). Failure to execute is a zero-sum game—you leave empty handed (or worse)—whereas going after a slightly less attractive market, but one where you can get some wins under your belt, is progress in the right direction.

The relative importance of the *Can We?* may seem logical, but it's often overlooked by very smart people. Let me give you a brief, real-world example:

Our shareholders brought in a large, top-tier strategy consulting firm to help us prioritize our renewable energy strategy internationally. The basic question was: in which geographies and applications should we focus business expansion efforts? The team did a lot of great research around the question of *Should We?*—market size, growth, renewable energy trends, government subsidies, competitive landscape, etc. They built a truly impressive weighted-scoring model that incorporated these variables in order to rank dozens of "micro-markets" (a combination of geography and application). The opportunity that rose to the top of the list? Home and small commercial renewable energy storage in Nigeria—a large and growing market that was a great fit for our technology, void of key competitors.

All good, right? Unfortunately, they completely overlooked the *Can We?* in their analysis. Lots of issues surfaced when it came time to execute, but two "show stoppers" completely thwarted efforts to penetrate the market in a real way. First, due to a variety of logistical and regulatory challenges, it took nearly six months to get product from our plant in the US to the distributor's warehouse, creating serious quality issues for our product on arrival (batteries) as well as obvious cash flow issues for the distributor . . . that's if they were able to find hard currency to actually pay for product, which at the time, was extremely difficult. So even with sufficient demand, distributors simply couldn't pay for product in $USD. We seriously considered taking coffee in trade at one point.

Not quite the executable strategy we had hoped for. Let's dive into a little more detail on how you might be able to avoid the same mistake.

## Should We?

Like most frameworks, the answer to this question will very much be unique to each organization, but it basically boils down to how attractive a particular market is relative to others from a strategic standpoint. And while straightforward conceptually, market attractiveness will be dependent on your industry, objectives, and capabilities. Here are some typical dimensions to consider in this assessment (and how relative weightings might be impacted by unique company attributes):

- **Market Size**—Are you a small / niche player in a massive market (like telecom) or a large player in a niche market (like hot sauce)? If the former, sheer market size of say the UK vs. Turkey is probably less important than it is for the latter, where market size may vary dramatically from one country to the other based on local tastes. There's a lot of good thinking in the ether on determining market size, but here are a few concepts to keep in mind:
    - **TAM**—Total Addressable Market: This number represents all demand for a given product or service in a particular region
    - **SAM**—Serviceable Addressable Market: That proportion of the TAM that relates specifically to your product or service

> **SOM**—Serviceable Obtainable Market: The portion of the SAM that you can realistically capture

In calculating an addressable market, the inclination is to start with the total market size, reduce that to a SAM or SOM based on a few key assumptions, assume some market share number, and viola! you have your (usually massive) target market size. That approach, unfortunately, almost always overstates the real size of the opportunity (and smart investors/executives will see right through it).

Instead, I would recommend taking a bottom-up approach which should give you a much more realistic view of a market's potential as well as a roadmap for where to focus commercial efforts if/as you move forward. The obtainable market formula here is:

*# of potential customers \* price \* volume (on, say, an annual basis)*

Getting to that number can be hard, but the effort is worth it. Here's a real-world example to illustrate:

> We were engaged by a private equity firm that was in the final rounds of vying for a manufacturer of "physiological shoes"—a type of athletic shoes that claimed to also have therapeutic benefits when worn consistently. The US market potential posited by the sellers—this was a foreign brand entering the US—was massive based on broad assumptions about the athletic shoe market. As you can imagine, even just a small share represented huge upside for a potential buyer.

▷ We took a different, bottom-up approach, focused on how many retail outlets would potentially carry the shoe ('customers'), how many potential pairs each retail 'door' in various channel segments represented, and scenarios around the ultimate retail price retailers could achieve (and corresponding wholesale prices) based on competitive offerings in the space. We combined this with some analysis around the number of people that fit the target customer based on gender, age, style, health issues, and geography. The outcome was a much more realistic (and orders of magnitude smaller) obtainable market than the one promoted in the investor deck. Our client ultimately passed on the acquisition, but had they gone forward, it would have also had a nice roadmap for the target's management team on where to focus business development efforts as they entered the US market.

► **Market Growth**—Similarly, market growth will be much more important to some businesses than others. If you're a $50M US company, you're probably OK with 2% annual market growth in a $4 billion market. Growth potentially becomes much more important in a smaller, or newly established market, particularly if even a significant share at the current size wouldn't move the dial in terms of meeting strategic objectives.

► **Competitive Landscape**—How fragmented is the market? E.g., is share concentrated in a government-owned entity that has established major barriers to entry? Are there other domestic players that have an already established local presence (not necessarily a bad thing) and what can you discern from their track record? Is there room for one more player, and how will you position your offering accordingly? Regardless of the landscape, if you don't offer any clear competitive differentiator, it's likely a non-starter.

- **Economics**—What does pricing and margin look like in potential international markets? A particular market could be huge and growing, but can you actually make money selling into it? As will be discussed a bit later, understanding your true "added cost" (all the incremental costs that build on your export price), as well as cost to serve (all the incremental overhead costs incurred to serve the customer), is a critical consideration here—duties and taxes are important but not the only key factors to consider.

- **Risk**—Risk can be seen as either a binary issue (i.e., past a certain point, no level of market attractiveness will be sufficient) or in shades of gray to be assessed with other factors. Regardless of your methodology, it's a critical element in determining whether or not (or how) to enter new a market. Here are the key buckets of risk that will need to be addressed in the planning process:

    ▷ **Currency**—How volatile is the currency relative to $USD? How sensitive is your business plan to this volatility?

- **Political**—How stable is the market politically? E.g., is there even a small risk of nationalizing (i.e., taking over) foreign business entities?

- **Business**—Can your contracts be enforced in local courts? Could local regulations thwart our brand/product positioning in the market? (see Walmart example discussed earlier)

- **Economic**—How stable is the local economy? Is your business plan susceptible to potentially high unemployment rates, inflation, etc.?

- **Strategic**—Can entry into a particular market backfire strategically (e.g., cause potential damage to the brand by manufacturing in China when it's a sector where "made in the USA" is particularly important)?

- **IP**—Are key elements of your intellectual property at risk by entering country X? Are there dependable ways to protect IP both on the front end (e.g., trademark registration) or if breached (e.g., timely litigation)?

For reference, Coface provides an excellent free service on their site to get a high level view of risk based on "Country Risk" and "Business Climate" (https://www.coface.com/Economic-Studies-and-Country-Risks), as well as a function that allows you to compare several countries side by side. See example below, comparing Argentina with Brazil:

| | BRAZIL | ARGENTINA |
|---|---|---|
| POPULATION | 208.5 million | 44.6 million |
| GDP PER CAPITA | 8,959 US$ | 11,658 US$ |
| COUNTRY RISK ASSESSMENT | C | D |
| BUSINESS CLIMATE ASSESSMENT | A4 | B |
| WATCH | | |
| STRENGTHS | • Varied mineral resources and agricultural harvests<br>• Large population (estimated at 211.9 million)<br>• Well-diversified industry<br>• Strong foreign exchange reserves (import coverage of roughly 26 months)<br>• Net creditor in foreign currency | • Major agricultural player (notably soya, wheat and corn)<br>• Large shale oil and gas reserves<br>• Education level higher than the regional average<br>• GDP per capita above the region's average<br><br>Major agricultural player (notably soya, wheat and corn)<br>Large shale oil and gas reserves<br>Education level higher than the regional average<br>GDP per capita above the region's average |
| WEAKNESSES | • Sensitive fiscal position<br>• Infrastructure bottlenecks<br>• Low level of investment (roughly 15% of GDP)<br>• Relatively closed to foreign trade (exports + imports represent only 22% of GDP)<br>• High cost of production (wages, energy, logistics, credit) harming competitiveness<br>• Shortage of qualified labour, inadequate education system | • Weak fiscal accounts and concerns over debt sustainability<br>• Capital controls were tightened, in order to curb dropping foreign exchange reserves<br>• Dependency on agricultural commodity prices and weather conditions<br>• Sticky and skyrocketing inflation and prohibitive interest rates level<br>• Bottlenecks in infrastructure |
| | View data for Brazil | View data for Argentina |

## Can We?

Once you've identified a short list of attractive target geographies based on *Should We?* criteria, the next issue is determining which markets you're in the best position to actually serve. By this I don't mean from the strategic sense of "ability to compete," but a hard look at the level of tactical implementation required—the mundane, day-to-day stuff that will ultimately determine success, regardless of how attractive the market. The requirements here will be very specific to the industry/company in question, but it's critical that you define a prioritized list of what will be needed to compete effectively and assess your capabilities accordingly.

For example, India could be the most attractive market available based on your *Should We?* analysis, but if you're unable to support growth because it would require 30 people fulltime to provide in country technical support, it's probably best to understand that now and focus elsewhere (or include the requirement as a key factor when comparing to other markets). Here are a few examples of *Can We?* dimensions that may impact how you view your ability to effectively serve a particular market:

- ▶ **Personnel**—Do we need to hire in country, and if so, how easy/difficult will that be from an HR and compliance standpoint? Note different countries have vastly different rules relating to hiring employees and the consequences of doing so for tax and other purposes.

- ▶ **Product Modifications**—Do we need to make major/expensive modifications to our current product to meet local requirements, either by law or to effectively compete against local alternatives?

- ▶ **Channels**—Do we have access to key channels/distributors to gain share (or are they already in exclusive distribution relationships with key competitors)?

- ▶ **Regulatory**—Is there an onerous regulatory process required to conform to local standards? Is that regulatory process mired by corrupt practices that are ubiquitous in certain markets?

- ▶ **Marketing**—Is English collateral acceptable, or do we need to translate all our marketing material (including our website content) into the local language?

As you move through this process, I would suggest viewing the *Should We?* as a binary metric—i.e., does the market reach a certain level of attractiveness to be in play? Then, prioritize this subset of markets based on key *Can We* criteria? Everything else being equal, I'd rather enter a smaller market with a higher likelihood of operational success, particularly in the early days of international expansion, than the other way around.

One final note: this exercise is not usually done in a vacuum. For example, you may have an OEM customer in the US that has a growing presence in Japan, Germany, and Brazil. Because of your customer's expansion into those markets, you're expecting aftermarket demand to grow in the next year or so as components parts (your business) need to be replaced. So, where to plant the flag? That's where a framework such as this—one that balances market attractiveness with your ability to execute—should help prioritize expansion efforts as well as bring focus to what needs to be in place operationally to execute on your growth plans.

CHAPTER FIVE

# Using Competitive Data

Analyzing existing export data for your offering is a good place to start in narrowing your initial focus to a manageable set of countries/regions. If you're operating in the US, a good, free resource for this exercise is the US Census Bureau (https://usatrade.census.gov/), where you can search merchandise export volume by a range of variables including commodity/HS-Code (international standardized system to classify traded products), year, region, country, and port.

The best way to illustrate how this might work is with a live hypothetical:

Suppose you're a specialty chocolate bar manufacturer assessing potential opportunities for expanding abroad. The company has some business in both Mexico and Canada but has spent very little time proactively pursuing growth overseas. You have a pretty good sense of which countries are the leading producers of chocolate, as well as which countries are major consumers, but the key question here is what countries are likely buyers of *American-made* chocolate bars?

Yes, there may be some huge undiscovered pocket of demand out there, but chances are, the market is fairly efficient and you can take current export volume as a proxy for which markets currently represent the universe of possible targets (incorporating a range of factors such as cost, duties, tastes, channels, etc.).

Using the Census Bureau online search tool, you can run a query for total exports by year/country for HS-Code 180690—*Chocolate and other food preparations containing chocolate*. Here's what you'd find for the top 25 export destinations (real data sorted by country, largest to smallest in volume) in pre-COVID 2019:

| Time | 2014 ($USD) | 2019 ($USD) | 2019 % of Total | Cumulative Total | 5-year CAGR |
|---|---|---|---|---|---|
| Canada | 306,003,113 | 326,832,867 | 32.4% | 32.4% | 1.3% |
| Mexico | 151,261,442 | 100,800,727 | 10.0% | 42.3% | -7.8% |
| Korea, South | 44,263,630 | 46,489,654 | 4.6% | 46.9% | 1.0% |
| Vietnam | 7,393,470 | 38,532,036 | 3.8% | 50.7% | 39.1% |
| Philippines | 29,256,075 | 31,941,658 | 3.2% | 53.9% | 1.8% |
| Australia | 43,737,794 | 28,548,031 | 2.8% | 56.7% | -8.2% |
| United Kingdom | 17,594,836 | 27,329,752 | 2.7% | 59.4% | 9.2% |
| Japan | 34,345,604 | 26,940,912 | 2.7% | 62.1% | -4.7% |
| Taiwan | 19,924,194 | 25,875,620 | 2.6% | 64.7% | 5.4% |
| Hong Kong | 23,872,580 | 24,080,830 | 2.4% | 67.1% | 0.2% |
| China | 17,471,222 | 23,481,795 | 2.3% | 69.4% | 6.1% |

| Time | 2014 ($USD) | 2019 ($USD) | 2019 % of Total | Cumulative Total | 5-year CAGR |
|---|---|---|---|---|---|
| Singapore | 25,539,762 | 21,849,236 | 2.2% | 71.5% | -3.1% |
| Thailand | 4,341,218 | 19,376,832 | 1.9% | 73.5% | 34.9% |
| India | 4,538,693 | 19,368,187 | 1.9% | 75.4% | 33.7% |
| Saudi Arabia | 20,591,503 | 19,320,020 | 1.9% | 77.3% | -1.3% |
| Peru | 10,754,818 | 17,203,693 | 1.7% | 79.0% | 9.9% |
| United Arab Emirates | 23,054,425 | 16,980,553 | 1.7% | 80.7% | -5.9% |
| Indonesia | 6,476,631 | 16,905,605 | 1.7% | 82.3% | 21.2% |
| Colombia | 15,284,613 | 15,396,513 | 1.5% | 83.9% | 0.1% |
| Chile | 9,258,940 | 12,955,207 | 1.3% | 85.2% | 6.9% |
| Panama | 7,774,816 | 12,027,586 | 1.2% | 86.3% | 9.1% |
| Netherlands | 9,286,809 | 10,723,135 | 1.1% | 87.4% | 2.9% |
| El Salvador | 6,879,133 | 10,047,823 | 1.0% | 88.4% | 7.9% |
| Malaysia | 4,332,120 | 8,825,352 | 0.9% | 89.3% | 15.3% |
| Costa Rica | 6,034,144 | 8,546,814 | 0.8% | 90.1% | 7.2% |

**Chart:** *US Exports—HS Code 180690 ($USD)*

My key take-aways from this information would be:

► Total exports for 2019 were just over $1B

► Over 42% of that went to Canada and Mexico (in line with the theme discussed in the prior chapter)

► The top 25 countries represent 90% of the volume

Now for a few potential surprises:

- ▶ South Korea was number three and Vietnam was number four; together they represent nearly as much volume as Mexico
- ▶ The UK is the only European country in the top 10, and only one of two, with the Netherlands, in the top 25. Together, they represent less volume than Vietnam
- ▶ From a regional perspective, Asia Pacific clearly represents the most demand with about 80% of volume outside Canada and Mexico; this is followed by Latin America, then Europe
- ▶ From a growth standpoint, a couple markets stand out: India, Vietnam, Thailand, Indonesia (again, all Asian countries)

Interesting, but how this data might help inform your strategic thinking? My initial thoughts would be to consider:

- ▶ The cluster of demand in APAC might prompt a potential regional vs. country approach. For example, if we're looking to bring on a local sales rep, we'd probably want to find someone with experience in several of these key countries vs. someone accustomed to representing products in just one country.
- ▶ We might start thinking longer term about what could make a good hub for serving the region more holistically. E.g., could Vietnam potentially be a good place to manufacture down the road once a meaningful commercial presence is established? Or vice versa? Would this be a

good base to serve other ASEAN (Association of Southeast Asian Nation) countries duty free?

▶ India's position high on the list is also worth thinking about. Over the past five years, India has grown at a CAGR of nearly 34%. True, that is off a low baseline, but that kind of growth should prompt some questions: What has driven that growth? Is it the growing consumer classes we've been hearing about? One large entrant into the market? A new and growing channel? And how long will the market continue to grow? How large will our SOM be in five years? We may find the challenges on entering the Indian market far outweigh the upside, but it's worth including in the analysis going forward.

▶ Finally, this data should provide a shorter list on which to focus our *Should We?/Can We?* diligence. Are certain markets already saturated? Is the growth in Vietnam sustainable? Is our key domestic competitor already selling into any of these countries? Do we have a distribution partner here in the US that can also serve us in say, Indonesia? In which countries would we need to re-label core products (an involved, time-consuming, and expensive process)?

## GOOGLE TRENDS

Google Trends is another free tool that may help you gain some insight into which countries might be receptive to your product or service. The core functionality allows you to get detailed search trends on any key word of interest. So, in our example of the chocolate bar manufacturer, we might use Trends to add context to our findings on exports by analyzing the use of the "Chocolate Candy" keyword over the past 12 months. Here's what you'd find in January of 2021:

**Chart:** *Relative Ranking by Country*

Given what we know about exports, how might we interpret this data?

- ▶ The number one region over the past 12 months was the United Arab Emirates. This may indicate relatively high demand, but UAE doesn't have a large export volume from the US. So, is there a fairly large market in UAE, but the preference is for other sources of chocolate like Belgium? Is there demand for American brands but high tariffs or other structural barriers limit volume? Will this change going forward? If there's significant unmet demand can you license your brand and unique recipe to a local manufacturer?

- ▶ Three of the five top countries are located in Asia, matching our hypothesis from export data that we should probably start narrowing our focus to this region. That said, Singapore at number two with a population of only about six million definitely caught my eye. Yes, the Philippines bought 50% more in US exports than did

Singapore, but with a population 15 times greater than Singapore. Since our hypothetical chocolates are a premium offering, would we be better off entering a smaller, higher-income market like Singapore, even if overall volume is lower? From an ease of doing business standpoint, Singapore is near the top of the list. How big of a factor should that be in our decision-making?

## OTHER SOURCES FOR COMPETITIVE/ MARKET INFORMATION

There are dozens of free/online resources that can help you triangulate into a manageable list of potential destinations. We've summarized and categorized many of these resources here (www.terrafirmastrategy.com/resources/terralinks) but here a few that I've found particularly useful:

- **International Trade Administration, Industries Reports** (www.trade.gov/industries-0)—Great source of free reports and data on roughly 20 different industry sectors such as Aerospace and Defense, Media & Entertainment, and Energy. Within each sector heading, you can find a variety of reports and expert analysis on a range of relevant topics, including country level industry dynamics.

- **International Trade Administration, Country Commercial Guides** (www.trade.gov/ccg-landing-page)—Another great source of free information that can be found at www.trade.gov. Each country guide contains a wealth of information for doing business in that country including Customs, Regulations & Standards, Trade and

Project Financing, Business Travel, and Leading Sectors for US Exports and Investments.

- ▶ **Competitor Websites**—An obvious but often overlooked source for where your competitors are playing abroad is publicly available information on their website. A few clicks under their "dealer network" or "where to buy" can be incredibly telling as to their level of commitment to international opportunities (is there just a generic email address for "international sales" or different country offices?) as well as regional/country level focus. A competitor's site may even include potential contact information for local distributors.

- ▶ **NationMaster** (www.nationmaster.com)—A site that aggregates public information from sources around the globe, NationMaster is a great one-stop shop for all things statistical. Whether you're looking for data on a particular sector or statistics to help back into a market size or proxy for demand, NationMaster is an incredibly useful free online resource.

CHAPTER SIX

# FDI/Investing

Technically, Foreign Direct Investment (FDI) is an investment made by a firm or individual in one country into business interests located in another. There are a variety of forms FDI may take, but this usually plays out with US-based companies establishing foreign business operations or acquiring assets (>10% investment) in another country. Every year, tens of billions of dollars are invested by US companies in international operations. In 2019, US outflows of FDI exceeded $156B.

FDI should be a consideration in your expansion plans because just about every foreign government offers various incentives for attracting FDI to its country. These incentives may not be the key driver in where to invest but could certainly be a factor influencing your decision on the margin. And even if a decision on where to go is clear, you don't want to leave potential money on the table by not being aware of available FDI incentives.

FDI typically falls into three major buckets:

- **Horizontal**—A domestic business establishing the same type of business in a foreign country. For example, when Nike opens a company-owned retail store in a new market like Ukraine.
- **Vertical**—A domestic business establishing or acquiring a related or supporting business in a foreign county. For example, our hypothetical US chocolate manufacturer acquiring a cocoa plant in Brazil.
- **Conglomerate**—A domestic business entering a completely new vertical in a foreign market. For example, if a US private equity fund bought a Canadian glassware manufacturer.

As a general rule, I would advise keeping your physical footprint as light as possible for as long as possible. Establishing a legal presence in a foreign market can be expensive and complex. It can also be much easier than exiting. In addition, adhering to all the legal and financial requirements in the interim can be a serious drain on management team time and company assets.

Referenced earlier, an especially helpful resource in evaluating the relative ease or difficulty of operating in various countries is The World Bank's Ease of Doing Business rankings (www.doingbusiness.org/en/rankings). The site has a ton of other useful information, but the rankings provide a great snapshot of where most every country worldwide ranks in terms of:

- ▶ Starting a business
- ▶ Dealing with construction permits
- ▶ Getting electricity
- ▶ Registering property
- ▶ Getting credit
- ▶ Protecting minority investors
- ▶ Paying taxes
- ▶ Trading across borders
- ▶ Enforcing contracts
- ▶ Resolving conflicts and insolvency

For example, if you plan on building a plant in Brazil, you should know that it ranks #170 out of 186 countries for dealing with construction permits. This may not be a make-or-break issue, but it's helpful to know up-front so you're able to plan for the relevant complexities from an investment, resources, and timing perspective.

## FDI INCENTIVES

Most countries offer incentives in an attempt to attract FDI. And while it won't likely be a critical factor in your decision-making, it's certainly worth taking the time and effort to learn what incentives are available in target countries because small differences can mean businesses either qualify or don't qualify under fairly technical rules. The range and value of incentives vary country to country, but these are some common themes to look for:

## Type of Incentive

▶ **General**—Customs duty and/or VAT tax waived on importation of equipment needed to build a plant/facility

▶ **Tax**—Reduction or elimination of range of taxes including corporate income tax, social security premiums (employees' or employers' portion), property tax, and consumption tax

▶ **Property/Infrastructure**—Land allocation, energy support, infrastructure support

▶ **Other**—Range of other incentives such as interest rate support, credit support, training support, stamp duty exemption, and purchasing guarantees

## Other Considerations

▶ **Minimums**—Most countries will require a minimum level of investment to qualify for various incentives, typically a relatively low number (e.g., well under ~$1M USD)

▶ **Geography**—Countries will often target incentives to certain regions such as underdeveloped provinces or free trade zones

▶ **Industry/Product**—Similarly, countries may offer additional or targeted incentives to further develop priority industries, promote strategic investment, or specifically focus on industries without a local production capability

Most countries have an office dedicated to promoting domestic investment from foreign companies. A simple Google search of "Foreign Investment + [name of country]" should point you in the right direction. In addition, most larger countries have resources based in the US that are more than happy to speak with you and explain what incentives might exist based on your company's size, business sector, and business objectives.

CHAPTER SEVEN

# Trade Agreements

International trade agreements are complex. There are hundreds of active agreements in place today among individual countries, trade blocks, and economic unions. The content of these agreements covers dozens of trade-related issues and are usually mired in political posturing, often spanning years of negotiations. On top of that, the current rise in fanaticism around the dueling philosophies of both nationalism and globalism make for a never-ending stream of media coverage highlighting either the evils or virtue of these agreements.

With all the noise and complexity surrounding trade agreements, it's easy to throw your hands up, put your head down, and just go about your business. That would be a mistake. While the talking heads on CNBC and FOX might focus on the unrelatable macro-economic impact of trade agreements—employment, GDP growth, trade balances, etc.—the fact is these agreements can have a direct impact on the bottom line of even the smallest US business and should certainly be a factor in strategic decision making.

## A BRIEF HISTORY FOR CONTEXT

The free trade era started with The General Agreement on Tariffs and Trade (GATT). The agreement was initially signed by 23 countries in October of 1947 with the overall purpose of promoting international trade by reducing or eliminating trade barriers, including tariffs and quotas. There were nine subsequent rounds of revisions culminating in the Uruguay Round (1986–1994) which established the World Trade Organization (WTO). The WTO became the successor to GATT and now has 164 member nations, with Liberia and Afghanistan joining in 2018. GATT and the WTO have had a major impact on tariff rates globally, which have decreased from around 22% on average in 1947 to around 5% today. Like GATT, the WTO is focused on the regulation of international trade between nations and the implementation, administration, and operation of covered trade agreements.

The number of agreements in force has accelerated dramatically over the past 20 years or so. In 1999, there were 69 active physical regional trade agreements in place. As of early 2021, there are 293. The WTO estimates that about half of the world's goods (in value) now crosses borders on a duty-free basis under a trade agreement.

The terminology in trade agreements can get quite confusing, and terms are often used interchangeably, but for our purpose the key definitions to be aware of as they relate to the broad heading of "trade agreements" are as follows:

1. **Regional Trade Agreements**—The umbrella term for a variety of agreement types (defined below). RTAs are technically agreements on trade that establish a preferential, reciprocal regime. Free Trade Agreements (FTAs) fall into this category and are often used synonymously with RTAs.

2. **Preferential Trade Agreement (PTA)**—These may be a first step toward an FTA but are not technically an RTA according to the WTO. PTAs typically involve a unilateral decision (by developed country) under which one party accords another (usually developing country) preferential treatment in trade. Some goods are eligible for lower duty (the "positive list") vs. the Most Favored Nation (MFN) rate which, despite its name, is the standard tariff rates a country charges on goods and services.

3. **Unions**—There are a range of unions—customs, economic, currency, monetary—that take the concept of free trade one, two, or many steps further. The European Union is an obvious example with a shared currency, legislative body, monetary policy, etc., but there are a number of other unions that form to meet shared objectives by a regional bloc of countries, including the Gulf Cooperation Council, Central American Common Market, and the Eurasian Economic Union. Unions typically enter into trade agreements as a single party.

4. **Trade and Investment Framework Agreement (TIFA)**—A trade pact that establishes a strategic framework and principles for resolving trade disputes between party countries. The US has dozens of active TIFAs with various countries ranging from Liberia to Kuwait to Mongolia.

5. **Bilateral Investment Treaty (BIT)**—An agreement between countries establishing terms and conditions for FDI by nationals of either party. The US currently has BITs in place with 42 countries around the world.

# THE US TODAY

As of this writing, the US has 14 "free trade" agreements in place with the following trading partners: Australia, Bahrain, Chile, Colombia, Israel, Jordan, Morocco, Oman, Panama, Peru, Singapore, South Korea, and multilateral agreements USMCA (formally NAFTA) and CAFT-DR (Central America and DR). There are many more being negotiated which can be found here (https://en.wikipedia.org/wiki/United_States_free-trade_agreements). The Office of the United States Trade Representative (USTR) is part of the Executive Office of the President and responsible for developing and recommending trade policy to the president as well as conducting trade negotiations at bilateral and multilateral levels.

## USMCA / NAFTA

NAFTA was far and away the most impactful trade agreement for the US and has been a hot topic in the news recently, as it was replaced by the United States-Mexico-Canada Agreement (USMCA) in July 2020. Depending on the political perspective in play, some consider USMCA a complete overhaul of NAFTA while others claim it makes just minor tweaks but leaves the general framework in place, both in terms of intent and content. Putting politics aside, the main differences are as follows:

- ▶ Higher pay for auto workers—starting in 2020, 30% of production must be done by workers earning at least $16 per hour (rising to 40% in 2023). The likely result will be a shift of job production from Mexico to the US.
- ▶ Canada will ease restrictions on its dairy market allowing US farmers to export $650 million in dairy products (about 3.5% of Canada's $16 billion dairy industry).
- ▶ Rules of Origin (discussed below) on automobiles increases from 62.5% to 75% (qualifying the maker for zero tariff). Again, likely shifting some manufacturing back to the US. In addition, 70% of the steel and aluminum used in vehicles will have to come from the US, Canada, or Mexico.

## Rules of Origin

A key concept in most RTAs is Rules of Origin (ROO), which determines the national source of a product, and therefore, eligibility for reduced tariff rates defined in the trade agreement (or just eligibility for import if there are restrictions on certain types of goods). For US exporters, goods qualify or "originate" if they are wholly obtained in the territory of a party to the FTA, or if they meet defined criteria on limits of "foreign content" in the product in question. While the concept is universally recognized as it relates to RTAs, there is a wide degree of variation in how the rules are applied from one government to the next (and there is no specific provision in GATT). ROOs are defined in the agreement by HS product code. Be sure to clearly understand the rules, and corresponding documentation requirements, before making commercial decisions based on potentially reduced tariff rates.

## SO, WHAT DOES ALL THIS MEAN FOR YOUR BUSINESS?

1. **Target Markets**—The most obvious advantage of trade agreements is the potential for reduced tariffs on export to partner countries. Selling to Australia at zero tariff against a competitor that is paying say, 10%, gives you a built-in pricing advantage that you can use to either increase margins, reduce price (to drive volume) or a combination of both. In addition to the direct impact on duties, FTAs typically seek to also facilitate trade via reduced red tape, common platforms, and dispute resolution mechanisms. Everything else being equal, particularly for smaller businesses, trading with member countries can be a good way to get your feet wet in international markets.

   One note here: depending on the agreement and product in question, administration costs can quickly add up and in some cases, make the benefit of reduced tariffs under FTAs simply not worth the effort. Ensure you fully understand all that's involved and weigh that against the relative benefit before making any major strategic decisions based on reduced tariffs.

2. **Supplier Decisions**—As discussed earlier, Rules of Origin typically require that a certain percentage of a product's components be sourced from a qualifying territory (either the country itself or a member country of a particular bloc). Think strategically about source of supply and how that might impact qualification for various FTAs. Paying a little bit more for local supply of key components, for example, may make sense if it's the difference between your buyer paying zero duty under an FTA or a standard MFN rate of 10 or 20%.

3. **Expansion Planning**—A range of commercial criteria naturally comes into play when considering expanding abroad. Proximity to customers, production costs, local talent, and raw materials are just a few. A deep analysis of impact on tariffs paid by buyers, while often an afterthought, should be a major part of strategic discussions as well. Will the intended location potentially reduce tariffs for current buyers in existing geographies, thereby increasing margins? Conversely, if your new plant is in a country not party to existing FTAs, will reduction in production costs be offset by the fact that buyers will now need to pay higher tariffs? Be sure to consider the impact of current (and in process) trade agreements in any analysis of the cost and benefits of expanding capacity overseas.

4. **Competitive Positioning**—Are you selling into a country under preferential tariff structure vs. a foreign competitor subject to higher tariffs? Might this change with a negotiated RTA between your export market and your overseas competitor? Mapping how you and your overseas competitors

might be impacted by evolving trade agreements requires some thoughtful analysis and "real time" research since trade arrangements can change frequently.

## A FEW HELPFUL RESOURCES:

1. **WTO Regional Trade Agreements Information System (RTA-IS)**—Provides a wide range of information on trade agreements searchable by country/territory and criteria/topics. It also provides an overview of the agreements themselves as well as links to the actual text of each agreement reported to the WTO. (http://rtais.wto.org/UI/PublicMaintainRTAHome.aspx)

2. **The FTA Tariff Tool**—Allows a user to search tariff information by HS code for all products covered under US FTAs. The tool can also help you determine eligibility for preferential rates by providing product-specific rules of origin. (https://beta.trade.gov/fta)

3. **Office of the US Trade Representative**—Provides an overview of all US FTAs along with trade detail and statistics with dozens of countries around the world. (https://ustr.gov/trade-agreements/free-trade-agreements)

SECTION THREE
# HOW

*Once you have a good sense of where you should be, and why, the critical question becomes **How?** This is the execution layer that will make or break any effort to expand abroad, no matter how much strategic thinking or thoughtful planning has gone into the exercise.*

*This section covers what I believe to be the primary drivers of tactical success from the commercial perspective. That said, even if your goal is more targeted, say to build a plant overseas, this section should help highlight ways in which that initiative might impact the broader business as a whole.*

CHAPTER EIGHT

# Business Models

How you enter a market can be as important as which market, and why. Having a clear view of the relative risks, rewards, required investment, management burden, and company capabilities of various options is critical to making the right decision here. In this section we'll review various options, and the pros and cons of each. Before we get into the details, however, it's important to keep a few key principles in mind as you work through this critical step implementing your global growth strategy:

1. Working through independent third parties—such as sales reps, distributors, and licensees—can be a low cost, low risk, relatively "easy" way to enter a new market abroad. (Note: you'll still be subject to some local legal requirements even if just using third parties.)

2. Company-owned facilities, while providing higher levels of control, also involve much greater risk at a much higher cost.

3. Especially early on, minimize your physical footprint to the extent possible. It can be much easier to grow into a market than exit—e.g., why establish a local legal entity if you can set up a lighter touch rep office?

4. With the previous point in mind, seek professional legal help in determining the best in-country approach from a legal entity standpoint. Be aware that some countries and localities have rules that a US perspective might find counter-intuitive, such as "goodwill indemnity" mentioned earlier. Experienced legal help can be expensive but is necessary.

5. Think long term—the optimal business model in a particular country will evolve over time. Don't lock yourself into long-term arrangements you might quickly outgrow.

6. Independent agents are considered an extension of your organization from a risk and compliance standpoint overseas. Ensure you have the right safeguards in place (e.g., anti-corruption language in agreements, etc.).

Below is a table outlining standard market entry models and some food for thought in terms of the pros and cons of each. This is not a fully exhaustive list, but these are the most common and should serve as a good starting point for determining what approach might be best for your business.

BUSINESS MODELS | 81

| MODEL | DESCRIPTION | PROS | CONS |
|---|---|---|---|
| Sales Reps | • Independent party with authority to market and sell product in defined territory<br>• Typically involves a commission on revenue received by company for orders placed via sales reps | • Company does not need an office or other entity in country<br>• Relatively easy/low cost to get started<br>• Limited ongoing overhead/expense | • May be difficult to control/manage remotely<br>• Termination may be complicated or costly (e.g., good will indemnification, referenced above)<br>• Potential for channel conflict |
| Independent Distributors | • Company appoints independent third party to act as distributor in defined country/territory<br>• Distributor purchases and resells product<br>• May be appointed on exclusive or non-exclusive basis | • Same as above +<br>• Distributor may provide other services including warehousing, delivery, marketing, warranty support, localization, etc. | • Same as above +<br>• Distributor owns relationship with customer |
| Value Added Reseller (VAR) | • Independent, local entity that purchases, modifies, and resells your products in the local market<br>• Can be exclusive or non-exclusive | • Same as above +<br>• Ready access to potential end users/customers<br>• VAR may enhance product to meet local competitive requirements | • Same as above +<br>• May require material engineering/product development support |
| Direct to Consumer | • Company sells products directly to end users on ecommerce platforms<br>• without use of third-party intermediaries (e.g., sales from website, telemarketing, direct mail) | • Can reach broad audience at relatively low levels of investment | • Product fulfillment, localization, and regulatory compliance can be a challenge<br>• Hard to drive significant levels of volume |

| MODEL | DESCRIPTION | PROS | CONS |
|---|---|---|---|
| **Direct to Consumer— Third Party Platform** | - Company lists products with ecommerce platforms such as Amazon and eBay | - Company can leverage reach of global platforms to reach potential customers all over the world | - Product fulfillment, localization, and regulatory compliance can be a challenge<br>- Hard to drive significant levels of volume |
| **Channel Partner** | - Independent, local entity that typically sells products used in conjunction with company's core products<br>- Partner sells company's product/service in combination with its own offering<br>- Can be exclusive or non-exclusive | - Same as above +<br>- Typically requires dealing with a relatively sophisticated commercial partner | - Same as above +<br>- May need to work through complex branding issues |
| **Local Retail** | - Company sells at wholesale price levels directly to local retail<br>- Company does not need a physical presence in country<br>- Can be exclusive or non-exclusive relationship | - Relatively low-cost way to enter a market<br>- Customer can assist with product localization requirements<br>- Company maintains control over product branding | - May be difficult to manage retail channel (e.g., product placement, display, etc.) remotely<br>- Risk of returned product if low sell through |

# BUSINESS MODELS | 83

| MODEL | DESCRIPTION | PROS | CONS |
|---|---|---|---|
| **Direct Foreign Presence in Country** | - 100% Company-owned facility in country<br>- Can take many forms, e.g., sales office, plant, distribution center, technical support, etc. | - Company has tight control over establishing its presence and managing local employees, activities, brand, etc.<br>- Communicates level of commitment to local market/potential customers<br>- Many strategic advantages including putting company closer to the customers, better understanding local competitive environment, and building a dedicated/loyal employee base<br>- Potentially more profitable if executed well | - Significant commitment and investment of time, money, and effort<br>- Working capital requirements<br>- High level risk including strategic, brand, execution, and financial<br>- Managing employees abroad can be highly challenging from both a cultural and regulatory compliance standpoint<br>- Can be very hard to unwind if needed |
| **Combination—Regional HQ + local presence** | - Company establishes regional center to build and manage commercial and / or operational activities in local countries<br>- In country approach can take any of the forms outlined above (i.e., independent reps, company-owned sales office, etc.) | - Puts management closer to local marketing, sales, and localization and customer support activities<br>- Communicates higher level of business commitment to regional customer base | - Depending on scope/type of entity, cons can be similar to those listed above |
| **Joint Venture with Local Partner** | - Company establishes a presence in concert with a local partner<br>- JV can be 50/50, minority, or majority-owned by company | - Partner has "skin in the game," increasing motivation for success<br>- Company can leverage partner's local knowledge, increasing chance of success<br>- Reduced/shared risk | - Can be complex and costly to implement and manage<br>- Requires high levels of time, energy and focus from Company management team |

| MODEL | DESCRIPTION | PROS | CONS |
|---|---|---|---|
| Licensing | - Company enters into licensing agreement with foreign partner, who pays Company royalty (typically a percent of revenue) on licensed product/services sold in country<br>- Scope of licensing agreement can cover specific countries, regions, verticals, or a combination of the above | - Potentially powerful combination of Company's unique value proposition with local brand, channel, or operational advantages of partner company<br>- Means to enter a market without establishing a local footprint | - Can be complex and costly to implement and manage<br>- Royalty rates often require very high levels of volume for real financial upside<br>- High levels of IP risk, which can be difficult to enforce abroad |
| Franchising | - Form of licensing where Company grants rights to franchisee to operate Company's proprietary business within a given territory<br>- Typically involves combination of franchise fee and ongoing royalties on revenue for use of brand, trademarks, trade dress, business model, proprietary processes, etc.<br>- Can cover individual franchisees or regional developers (who may open own units or sub-franchises) | - Allows company to expand internationally with lower levels of risk<br>- Company maintains control over branding and key business processes | - Requires a high degree of company oversight<br>- IP risk<br>- Need scale for material financial benefit to Company |
| Acquisition of a Local Business | - Company acquires a local entity as a means to enter a market | - Quick way for Company to establish a local presence with full management control<br>- Can be good way to execute targeted market entry strategy | - Many acquisitions, even in the US, fail to meet value-creation expectations; this risk only increases overseas |

CHAPTER NINE

# Finding New Customers

Whether you're just starting to export, or already have a healthy business overseas, you're likely on a never-ending hunt for new customers. There's no single "right approach" but employing the right combination of tactics described below can have a dramatic impact on the speed and likelihood with which you're able to meet your business objectives in international markets.

## TRADE SHOWS

I'm not a huge fan of trade shows generally. They feel to me like an archaic holdover from the "old" way of doing business. Put your wares on a table and wait for people to come around and place orders. That said, if employed strategically, international trade shows can certainly be an effective way to find new customers.

A good source for searching trade shows overseas by industry, country, etc. is The Trade Show News Network (https://www.tsnn.com/index.php). These events can be a major investment for a company of any size, so if you're going to spend the time and money, ensure you take the right actions to maximize your return:

► **Pre-work: Don't be reactive**—Most of the 'leads' that walk into your booth are not likely customers at all, but rather potential suppliers on a sales mission, or competitors fishing for information. Set up meetings ahead of time with a handful of target customers and prepare custom pitches. These one-on-one discussions will most likely yield better results than the random walk-in.

► **Collect and process leads**—The comment above notwithstanding, you never know who might be a future customer. With all the frenetic activity surrounding a trade show, legitimate leads can easily fall through the cracks. Set up a structured process with the team to systematically collect, disseminate and follow up on all leads. There are dozens of automated tools/apps that can help with this process.

► **Make a schedule**—Go to any trade show and you'll typically see a bunch of employees of the exhibitor standing around talking to each other—obviously not a great use of time or money. Develop a detailed schedule of when people from your team need to be in the booth—otherwise they should be in scheduled meetings, attending or giving presentations, or walking the floor to gather competitive intel or make contact with potential partners.

- **Walk the floor**—Think about who else will be exhibiting and how they might be able to help you with your business development objectives. This could include:

  ▷ Competitors that you might be able to partner with in certain geographies

  ▷ Players in adjacent categories who you could work with on an integrated solution, or who could help make an introduction to a common distributor

  ▷ OEMs or VARs (Value-added Resellers) that use your product either directly or indirectly

Check the directory beforehand to see who else will be there and identify 10-20 potential targets to pursue. Set up meetings ahead of time, but if that's not possible, take advantage of being under one roof to get the conversation started.

- **Go to where your customer is**—Going to your customers' physical exhibits can be a more effective and less costly way of finding new customers. Think of it as a captive audience you can corner in their booth! Identify where your targets will be and when you can go find them—don't wait for them to find you.

- **Gather intel**—Trade shows can be a treasure trove of competitive intelligence, but you're not going to find it in your booth. Include time on the master schedule for people to walk the floor and collect helpful information—pictures of booths, brochures, new product launches, product positioning, training information, etc. Encourage the team to have informal conversations with your competitors and schedule time afterwards to share what they've learned.

- ▶ **Check the ROI**—Exhibiting at trade shows is expensive. The direct costs are obvious—booth design, exhibition costs, travel, etc.—but the opportunity cost of preparation and time taken from other value-added activities can make a direct ROI on the effort difficult to justify. Calculate the total cost and what metrics will need to be met in order to realize a positive ROI on attendance in the first place.

When determining ROI, be specific. Return can represent hard revenue targets—e.g., we're investing $100K so our breakeven/target in new business is $300K— or some/all objectives can be more qualitative in nature—such as media exposure, lead generation, brand awareness, or a platform for a new product launch. Whatever metrics you use, set specific targets that will justify the effort and track the results. Doing so will not only help determine if the investment was worth it, but it will also bring much needed focus to planning and activities while at the show.

## GOVERNMENT RESOURCES

In addition to trade shows, there are a variety of other sources that can be employed to find customers/partners abroad:

- **International Trade Administration**—The US government has a whole department focused on helping US companies expand globally: The International Trade Administration, found at www.trade.gov. I highly suggest you take the time to click around the website as there are a ton of helpful resources, reports, and tools available free of charge. As it relates to finding customers, in particular, there are two programs you should absolutely consider (as described on the trade.gov website):

  - **The Gold Key Service**— *"Provides U.S. companies with matchmaking appointments with up to five interested partners in a foreign market. The full service includes identification and outreach to potential matching firms, sending client's information to identified matching firms, preparing a profile of interested firms, attending the appointments and providing a report with the profile and contact information for interested firms."*

  - **The International Partner Search**—*"Provides U.S. companies with a list of up to five partners/distributors that have expressed an interest in the client's goods/services. The service includes identification and outreach to potential matching firms, sending client's information to identified matching firms, preparing a profile of interested firms, and providing a report with the profile and contact information for interested firms."*

I've employed both these services in multiple contexts, and while results can vary by country, these services are a great example of our tax dollars at work. At the time of this writing, the Gold Key Service was ~$1,000 total for each country. Hard to beat.

▶ **Trade Missions**—Trade missions are organized by governmental agencies or industry groups with the express purpose of exploring international business opportunities. Trade missions will vary in form and purpose, but typically support business development efforts with:

▷ One-to-one meetings with foreign industry executives and government officials selected to match your specific business objectives

▷ Networking events with guests from local industry groups, including chambers of commerce, associations and relevant business councils

▷ Briefings and roundtables with the local legal and business community

▷ Site visits to local facilities where your technologies/services may be applied

▷ Media coverage

For a list of trade missions sponsored by the US Government, check out https://www.trade.gov/trade-missions-schedule.

## ADDITIONAL RESOURCES

▶ **Existing Partners**—Is yours a B2B business with customers already selling abroad? Are you supplying OEMs that need aftermarket support in other geographies? Are any of your key suppliers supporting competitors in foreign markets? Engage with your entire business ecosystem to not only gain intel on international opportunities but also to obtain leads on potential business contacts that can aid with your expansion plans.

▶ **International Financial Institutions**—There are dozens of entities that fall under the umbrella of International Financial Institutions, most with the mission of supporting economic development in the country or region in which they focus. Many contain searchable databases on their site where you can gather information on projects, grants, trends, or potential partners in your segment of interest. A good example is the Asian Development Bank's project database (https://www.adb.org/projects), containing close to 11,000 projects in various stages of approval.

▶ **Trade Leads Database**—The Trade Leads Database (https://www.export.gov/Trade-Leads), maintained by US Commercial Services, contains prescreened business leads and government tenders gathered around the world. You can search by vertical, product, country, etc. to get a list of opportunities that might be right for your business.

- **World Chambers**—The World Chambers Network (http://www.worldchambers.com) provides many services for international companies. In particular, with 12,000+ entries and over 40 million members, the official Chamber Directory can be a useful resource for establishing new business contacts as well as learning more about a particular market. Also browse the directory for relevant public trade shows and public tenders.

- **EXIM Bank**—The Export-Import Bank of the United States (EXIM) can be an extremely valuable resource for US exporters on a variety of levels. I strongly suggest you browse their site to learn about their full range of services (https://www.exim.gov/). Specifically, as it relates to finding and closing international buyers, EXIM's loan guarantees support US companies in securing competitive financing for creditworthy international customers.

CHAPTER TEN

# Pricing

How you approach pricing in international markets can make the difference between success and failure, particularly in the early days. The eBay Japan case cited earlier is a good example: the US-based transaction pricing model just didn't work in Japan. Japanese people were highly averse to paying a transaction fee for a service that had very little brand recognition in the local market. Unfortunately, like most other aspects of international business, pricing in foreign markets can be exponentially more complex than domestic pricing. In this chapter, we take a closer look at key factors that should be assessed when developing and executing an effective international pricing strategy:

## CORE BUSINESS OBJECTIVES

Explicitly defining your organization's objectives for its overseas business is a critical step in your international growth strategy, and how you approach pricing should be rooted in supporting that objective. For example, if your key goal is establishing a foothold in an international market as a long-term investment in business growth, then underlying pricing should reflect that objective with relatively aggressive penetration pricing. On the other hand, if exploiting a niche, premium segment in an international market is the goal, then initial price should seek to maximize gross margin and pricing discipline established to ensure pricing levels remain aggressive. When determining where you stand, consider the following high-level strategic objectives and the corresponding implications for international pricing:

- Increase unit volumes to drive down costs—aggressive penetration pricing
- Utilization of excess capacity—marginal cost unit pricing
- Increase gross margins—high pricing targeting premium sectors (with full understanding of loaded cost!)
- Generate gross margin dollars—optimized price/volume formula
- Establish strategic presence in key overseas market—targeted/aggressive penetration pricing

This may seem self-evident, but all too many companies either copy and paste their domestic price lists or react over aggressively based on the first order received by a foreign buyer (regardless of the long-term plan). The point here is to define your objectives first, then take the approach that will best support your strategic objectives and adjust as necessary.

## LOCALIZE PRICING

Pricing dynamics from country to country will vary dramatically. And, while it's natural to assume that price should generally correlate with relative country wealth (such as GDP per capita), that's not always the case. A good example of variation in international pricing is the (infamous) Big Mac Price Index, a comparison of the price of a Big Mac in various countries. As of July 2020, the most expensive Big Mac in the world could be found in Switzerland at $6.91—not surprising given the generally high cost of living in Switzerland. But what was number two? Surprisingly, Lebanon at $5.95 (ranked 23$^{rd}$ in cost of living vs. 2$^{nd}$ for Switzerland). What countries were in the bottom five? Mexico, Ukraine, Turkey, Russia, South Africa (at $1.86!) respectively—three of which (Mexico, Turkey, and Russia) have a significantly higher GDP per capita than Lebanon.

Yes, Big Mac pricing incorporates many factors other than strategic considerations, but the point here is to take a thoughtful approach to pricing in each market (again, with corporate objectives in mind). Price too high in a given country, for example, and you may lose volume; price too low, and you may be giving away margin unnecessarily or not fully capitalizing on perceived value.

## PARALLEL IMPORTS

A parallel import is a non-counterfeit product imported from another country without the permission of the intellectual property owner. How this typically plays out in reality is an unofficial in-country distributor competes with your exclusive/appointed channel partner by purchasing product from distributors in other countries. For example, a large domestic distributor that has preferential tier-one pricing may decide to dump excess inventory into Mexico at the end of the year at very low or even no margin just to meet volume targets.

Parallel imports can cause significant challenges for your international business. Firstly, parallel imports can be alienating and demotivating to official channel partners that have invested in growing the local market—only to have a competitor free ride on this work by selling against them. Secondly, this dynamic can also cause serious in-country pricing/brand positioning issues as official and unofficial channels compete for volume by undercutting each other. Thirdly, parallel importers can cause operational issues—who's going to support the warranty claim from a product sold by an unofficial distributor? And finally, parallel imports can drive down gross margins for the exporter. Total volume may not decrease but trading higher margin international sales for lower margin domestic volume (as in the Mexico example above), may do unforeseen damage to the business.

While parallel imports can be partly managed via commercial agreements—e.g., including a clause in a distribution agreement allowing for termination if a distributor sells outside its assigned territory(ies), eliminating major pricing anomalies between regional pricing levels can help negate the conditions for parallel importing. Buyers in Switzerland may not be able to buy Big Macs from South Africa, but if they could, saving $5 per burger would no doubt be a serious incentive. It's an efficient market—even what appears to be fairly innocuous differences in country pricing can motivate bad behavior. The trick here is localize pricing in an actionable and strategic manner while ensuring that all that good pricing work stays where it belongs—in the local market.

## LANDED COST

While not always a straightforward calculation, understanding your landed cost (including hidden and qualitative costs) is critical for several reasons. On the front end, it is an essential variable in understanding if/how well you'll be able to compete in a given geography. Even at relatively low gross margins, for example, will you be priced out of the market by the time your product hits your channels? Will there be enough margin on the table to incentivize your distributor to invest time and effort in moving your product? Secondly, taking all costs into account will provide an accurate view of real margins and ensure you're either passing on all relevant costs to customers, or identifying them and getting credit for your investment. Finally, a good view on landed cost will enable you to make strategic decisions about where you might be able to cut costs, and as a result, either improve margins or pass savings along to customers to grow volume (or a combination of both).

Landed costs allocations are often oversimplified to include a percentage cost "adder" for freight and duties, but there are many associated costs that should be accounted for as well. Many of these costs/fees can be nominal on their own but add up to a material amount in the aggregate. Consider the following when assessing landed cost:

> The basic formula for landed cost = **Shipping + Customs + Risk + Admin/Overhead**

## Shipping

- Crating—Specialized export pallets/crating requirements for international shipments
- Packaging—Additional costs of labelling/packaging to meet international requirements
- Handling—Any additional costs incurred from unique handling requirements
- Freight—Shipping cost from port of departure to destination port
- Inland Transport—Transport from destination port to customer's door/warehouse
- Pre-Export Inspections—May be required depending on product
- Pre-Carriage—Cost of moving product from the warehouse / factory to the port
- AES Fees—Costs involved with ensuring that Electronic Export Information (EEI) is correctly filed through the Automated Export System (AES)

## Customs

- Tariffs/Duties—Taxes (usually predefined % * Value) imposed by the destination country on imported goods *(Note: while often used interchangeably, a tariff is a % rate while a duty is a dollar amount)*

- Value-added Tax (VAT)—Tax levied in 160+ countries around the world at each stage in the supply chain (discussed in more detail below)
- Other Taxes and Fees—e.g., Consumptions Tax
- Brokers Fees
- Terminal Fees—Fees (such as unloading) charged at destination port
- Harbor Maintenance—Fees (usually a % of value) charged by importing port. For reference, in the US, harbor maintenance fee is 0.125% of the entered value
- International Documentation—Cost of providing required documentation for export, including bills of lading, bills of lading for FOB
- Inspection—Fees for shipment inspection at either port of departure or point of entry

## Risk

- Cargo Insurance—Additional insurance to the coverage provided by carriers, e.g., insuring gap risks such as "Acts of God," terrorism, strikes, riots, etc.
- Credit Insurance—Premiums for protection against non-payment by foreign buyers
- Compliance/Licensing—Indirect costs associated with acquisition of required licenses or other requirements for exporting to target country

- Safety Stock—Cost of carrying extra stock for potential supply disruptions, often required by foreign buyers
- FX—Cost of hedging against risk associated with exchange rate fluctuations (e.g., hedging if selling in foreign currency)

## Overhead

- Staff—Incremental staff required to handle international customer base (direct expense)
- Travel—Travel directly related to servicing international customers
- Due Diligence—Cost of screening potential new customers including third party reports, legal fees, and consultants
- Certifications—All costs associated with acquiring necessary certifications to sell in the target market
- Allocated SG&A—Cost allocation of SG&A to support the international business (indirect expense)
- Cost of Capital (terms)—Opportunity cost of carrying customer receivables

Put in the work up-front to understand landed cost, channel margins, and market price. Even if these numbers are estimates, having a detailed model will prove invaluable in negotiating pricing and sharing the margin pool in a way that will incentivize channel partners to generate volume while ensuring actual margin realization is sufficient to justify the time, effort, and capital investment in international development.

## VAT

The concept of a value-added tax (VAT) can be confusing to Americans, but more than 160 countries around the world use some form of value-added taxation. In short, a VAT is levied on gross margin at each stage in the supply chain, with a credit given once the goods are sold to the next buyer. Like a sales tax, the consumer ultimately bears the cost of the VAT. But unlike a sales tax, each player in the supply chain—from manufacturer to retailer—is on the hook for paying (then reclaiming) their portion of the tax as value is added along the way.

## EXCHANGE RATES

One of the most significant factors in international pricing (and corresponding margin realization) are exchange rates. Conventional wisdom is that, from an exporter's perspective, a weakening currency is good for volume since it effectively reduces the price to importing countries, thereby increasing demand. While this may be true in the short term, research from Jonathan Kearns and Nikhil Patel of the Bank for International Settlements (BIS), finds that at times a rising currency can actually be a stimulant to exports by supporting domestic investment and general economic activity, and a falling currency a depressant on exports.

While macro-economic theories may be interesting, the reality is that the impact on your particular business may fall in line with an expected empirical outcome, or more likely, given Murphy's Law, may prove the exception to the norm. And while some models may prove out at the macro level, individual businesses may be impacted in very different ways based on the exact same conditions. Here are key considerations as you tackle the issue of exchange rates and the implications for your business:

1. **Currency Pricing**—Most large, multi-national corporations have groups of professionals dedicated to determining invoicing, payments, and settlements strategy and managing the financial impact of fluctuations in exchange rates—the Treasury. Most small to mid-market exporters, on the other hand, do not have that luxury. Not having in-house professionals, however, doesn't reduce the importance to your business of taking a strategic view of whether you price/invoice in $USD or local currency (or an unrelated, neutral currency).

   At a high level, advantages of Producer Country Pricing (PCP)—i.e., pricing in your home currency—include simplicity, reduced exchange rate risk for the exporter, and lower transaction fees. Local Country Pricing (LCP)—i.e., pricing in the currency of your export market—can have distinct advantages as well, including shifting of exchange rate risk away from customers, marketing value (localization of offering) and pricing flexibility. What's best for your business? Considerations on best approach include:

   ▶ Relative transaction size (larger indicates LCP)
   ▶ Number of countries served (more indicates PCP)
   ▶ Nature of competition (local substitutes indicates LCP)
   ▶ Relative customer buying power (high indicates LCP)
   ▶ Industry standard (are you an outlier?)

Regardless of whether your business invoices in local currency today, currency pricing is one of those areas that can have a major impact on stability and profitability and should likely be assessed with the help of experts in the field. It's definitely worth time and investment (whether you're billed in dollars or yen!).

2. **Commodity/Input Prices**—Goods that have a high ratio of globally traded, indexed commodities often have a natural ballast when it comes to the impact of exchange rates on COGS, pricing, and ultimately your company's competitiveness from a pricing perspective. For example, in the lead acid battery industry, nearly two-thirds of the variable cost of finished goods comes in the form of lead. When the dollar weakens against a particular currency, lead becomes more expensive relative to competitors buying lead in the now stronger currency. To illustrate, if the US dollar weakens by 10% against the euro, the cost of goods for a US manufacturer relative to a European manufacturer, who is buying lead in euro on the open market, increases by ~6% (2/3*10%). Assuming this differential in lead is passed through to consumers in the form of margin-neutral price adjustments, a European buyer purchasing US-made batteries in USD will see an effective price decrease, but certainly much less than the 10% assumed by looking purely at exchange rate movements (4% in this case).

The same logic applies to other businesses as well, where key cost inputs are transacted in a non-$USD currency (say market research with a large payroll in India). The fundamental question remains, how is your cost structure impacted by the same movements in FX relative to your competition? Taking the time to build sound, dynamic models can take the guesswork out of FX movements, bring rationality to pricing decisions, and ensure real (vs. assumed) impacts are driving key commercial decisions.

3. **Competitive Dynamics**—Despite macro movements in exchange rates, and academic assessments of impact on exports, the most important factor in determining risks and opportunities around FX is your competitive landscape. Here it's important to assess your business on a regional level: who's your competition and how are they structured? Is your key competitor a US company that manufactures in China? Or is it a Chinese company that buys raw materials and manufactures in Europe...and in what currency do they invoice? Each situation will be unique, but outlining the impact of material FX movements on key competitors is a worthwhile exercise in determining your own moves.

To illustrate with another overly simplistic example, let's say a key US competitor of yours manufactures in China to support its Australian business (and you don't). With a material increase in $USD vs. Chinese RMB, your competitor will likely enjoy more pricing flexibility than you would exporting from the US to the same Australian market. So, setting price for your Australian business without accounting for this dynamic could put you at a competitive disadvantage.

Key questions to help frame your FX strategy include:

- How do FX movements impact your cost of goods relative to competitors?
- How does this impact effect relative price and margin? How should you adjust price accordingly?
- How do FX movements impact import costs relative to competitors from the customer perspective?
- Is your method of invoicing (PCP vs. LCP) based on a thoughtful strategy, or is it "just the way we've always done it"?

To sum up, there's a ton of insightful research available to help you better understand the potential impact of exchange rates on flows of international trade. At the end of the day, however, there is not an easy, one-size-fits-all answer, and some heavy lifting will be required to understand the practical implications of exchange rate movements on your particular business/industry.

CHAPTER ELEVEN

# Shipping and Collecting

Finding buyers abroad who are willing to pay your proposed price is hard, but just the first step in the commercial process. Getting your product to the intended location in acceptable condition, and then actually getting paid can be equally difficult. Here we cover some important concepts that can help streamline the process as well as reduce risk.

## FREIGHT FORWARDERS

A freight forwarder is a third party that coordinates the shipment of goods from one destination to another using a range of carrier types. Finding a reliable, experienced freight forwarder should be a top priority in your international expansion plans. Services offered by freight forwarders vary, but in general they:

- ▶ Serve as the go-between manufacturers and shippers for transportation of goods across international borders

- Negotiate with shippers to determine freight pricing
- Obtain insurance to protect goods during the transportation process
- Prepare necessary documentation to ensure goods can be transported internationally

Freight forwarders come in all shapes, sizes, and vertical groupings so it's important that you do your homework before partnering. Word of mouth is a great place to start, but there are also several public sources that can narrow your search, including the WCAworld website (https://www.wcaworld.com/Directory) and The National Customs Brokers and Forwarders Association of America. (https://www.ncbfaa.org/).

## INCOTERMS

If you're doing business internationally, you need to understand Incoterms irrespective of your function within the organization. Not only do Incoterms define your level of responsibility relative to the buyer in international transactions, if viewed strategically, the right Incoterm can be a source of competitive advantage, customer satisfaction, and even margin improvement.

Incoterms are a set of pre-defined commercial terms (not laws) developed by the International Chamber of Commerce and updated every 10 years. In short, they were created to standardize and clearly define each party's responsibilities in international commercial transactions, specifically the costs, risks, and business processing duties in delivery from buyer to seller (note that delivery here means transfer of goods, not necessarily when and where title changes hands).

More specifically, Incoterms define who owns risk, actions, and financial responsibility along the continuum of getting goods from point A (Seller) to point B (Buyer) including:

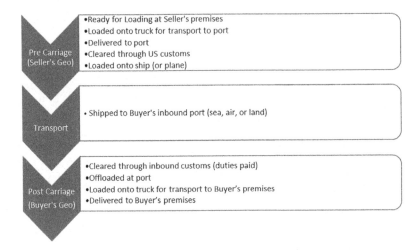

Incoterms 2020 is boiled down to 11 rules, represented by distinct three-digit codes. Seven apply to any mode of transportation, the remaining four only to transportation by water (as defined below). While not legal standards, Incoterms are now nearly universal in international trade and required for US custom documentation, commonly used in sales agreements, and standard language when dealing with just about any party along the supply chain.

## Summary of Incoterms 2020:

- ▶ **EXW (Ex Works)**—One of the simplest Incoterms, here the Seller makes goods available at its location; Buyer arranges for everything from pick-up onwards, including cost and freight management.

- **F Terms**—"Delivery" of goods consummated at some point on *Seller's* territory

  ▷ **FCA** (Free Carrier)—Seller delivers goods cleared for export at a pre-determined location. This location can be the Seller's own facility—similar to Ex Works but the Seller loads the goods onto Buyer's truck (common practice anyway). However, FCA can also mean that goods are delivered by Seller to Buyer's chosen place of delivery. Buyer is responsible for unloading and re-loading if delivered to a facility outside of Seller's control.

  ▷ **FAS** (Free Alongside Ship)—Relates only to transactions involving sea/waterway. Seller's responsibility includes all steps up to the point when goods are loaded onto a vessel, including delivery to terminal and customs formalities, but not including loading onto ship (Buyer's responsibility). Usually used (vs. FOB) when goods require special handling.

  ▷ **FOB** (Free on Board)—very common Incoterm, also applies to sea/waterway only. Seller is responsible for everything including loading onto ship. Note: Buyer cannot take possession until the bill of lading is surrendered. Seller must also arrange for export clearance. Buyer is responsible for cost of freight and all costs/activities thereafter.

- **C Terms**—Seller's responsibilities include all F-terms, *plus* cost of freight

  - **CFR** (Cost and Freight)—Seller delivers and covers all cost, including freight, up to a named port of destination. Applicable to transactions involving sea/waterway only. Risk transfers to Buyer when goods are loaded onto ship. Buyer is responsible for insurance, inbound customs, post carriage, etc.

  - **CIF**—Broadly similar to CFR but Seller is responsible for obtaining insurance while goods are in transit to named port of destination. Applicable to transactions involving sea/waterway only.

  - **CPT** (Carriage Paid To)—Essentially CFR but for non-containerized sea freight.

  - **CIP**—Essentially CPT, but like CIF, Seller is required to obtain insurance for goods while in transit.

- **D Terms**—Delivery of goods is consummated at some point in Buyer's territory

  - **DPU** (Delivered at Place Unloaded)—New Incoterm for 2020 that replaces DAT (Delivered at Terminal). Seller bears all costs and risks up to and including delivery at agreed upon location. Import clearance and all charges after unloading are the responsibility of Buyer, however, Seller is generally responsible for any delay/demurrage charges at destination terminal.

▷ **DAP** (Delivered at Place)—Seller is responsible for all costs/responsibilities of DAT plus delivery to Buyer's named destination, excluding customs costs and responsibilities at destination port, which remain the Buyer's responsibility.

▷ **DDP** (Delivered Duty Paid)—Essentially "door to door" delivery. Seller is responsible for all costs and risks including clearing customs in destination port, payment of duties, required documents, etc. Buyer has no risk or responsibility until goods are delivered (with the exception of unloading at named place of destination). Note: highest risk to Seller, use with extreme caution!

Below is a summary in broad terms of who owns what at each stage in the process for each Incoterm. Please note that Incoterms in bold are for sea freight only.

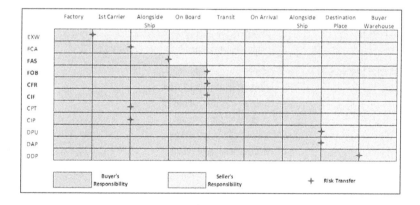

## Using INCOTERMS strategically

Incoterms are oftentimes an afterthought in international transactions, but if used strategically, they can be a powerful tool to achieve key business objectives. To illustrate, here are a few general examples of how to think about Incoterms in a more strategic context:

| Objective | Approach | Sample Term(s) |
|---|---|---|
| Reduce Complexity | Pass responsibility over to Buyer early in process | EXW, F Terms |
| Establish a Revenue Center | Manage freight through carriage and pass marked-up cost onto Buyer | C Terms, D Terms |
| Control Parallel Imports | Maintain ownership of process to point of goods loaded onto ship | FAS, FOB |
| Manage Customer Experience | Maintain ownership of process to point of delivery | CFR+ |
| Establishing Competitive Advantage | Pursue terms that provide incentives vis-à-vis domestic competitors | Depends |
| Manage Landed Cost | Manage shipping through carriage to negotiate better freight rates than individual customers; incremental savings can be passed on to drive volume, or retained to increase margins | CFR+ |
| Reduce Risk | Transfer responsibility to Buyer early in process | EXW |

A few final thoughts related to Incoterms:

1. Incoterms state when risk in goods passes from Seller to Buyer, but not title, which must be addressed separately.

2. Incoterms are not a substitute for a commercial agreement covering issues such as price, termination, territories, governing law, payment terms, etc.

3. Relative capabilities need to be considered when determining the right Incoterm to use, e.g., getting product through customs in a foreign country is usually better left to the buyer.

4. Always clearly specify which Incoterm and edition is being used, e.g., [Incoterm, delivery point]Incoterms® 2020

5. With the exception of CIF and CIP, Incoterms are generally silent on the matter of insurance, assuming that insurance moves with cargo responsibility based on the Incoterm being used. Ensure insurance terms are clearly defined before product is shipped.

6. Be sure you understand all fees and charges along the way from various parties, e.g., some carriers absorb terminal handling charges while others do not

7. Incoterms are complicated, when in doubt, seek guidance from a professional

## PAYMENT TERMS

One of the last hurdles in your commercial discussions/negotiations with potential customers abroad will likely be payment terms. There are many variations on getting paid, but the most common, from least to most risky are:

1. **Cash in Advance**—The buyer pays for goods before they're shipped. Receiving funds prior to shipping obviously addresses collection risk, but also addresses any exposure the parties may have to exchange rate fluctuations. Transaction costs are also kept to a minimum. Naturally buyers are typically opposed to cash in advance; it ties up capital in goods that aren't guaranteed to ship, at least on time.

2. **Letter of Credit (LCs)**—An LC is a commitment by a bank in advance of the transaction that payment will be made on behalf of the buyer when the terms and conditions stated in the LC have been met. The assessment of credit worthiness of the buyer is the responsibility of the bank, so the risk is essentially transferred from the buyer to the bank itself. LCs can be complicated to execute and relatively expensive, but the added level of protection can be worth the effort.

3. **Documentary Collections (DC)**—In a DC transaction, the buyer's and seller's bank work together to facilitate the transaction. The exporter prepares a Bill of Exchange that is forwarded to the Importer's bank via the Exporter's bank. The Bill of Exchange provides details on required documents, payment amount due, terms of payment, and timing of title transfer. The importer's bank releases required import documents and title to the Importer when terms are met, typically when payment is received in full (which is then forwarded to the Exporter's bank).

   DC does not guarantee payment like a letter of credit but can be a faster and cheaper to way to facilitate the transaction. Most importantly from a risk standpoint, in the case of non-payment by the importer, the exporter still owns the goods.

The exporter can either try to find another buyer in country or ship the product back to the country of origin for re-stocking. Yes, there is a cost, but the entire shipment is not at risk.

4. **Open Account**—Here, goods are shipped before payment is received from the importer, who typically has 30, 60, or 90 days in which to pay ("terms"). While providing credit to potential first-time customers can really help close a sale, the obvious risk here is that the buyer either doesn't pay or pays very late. I have found that many importers use credit as a de facto consignment arrangement, paying down their balance once they've imported and sold through inventory.

Many deals fall apart when it came to when and how the customer is going to pay for product. The fundamental issue here is risk. How much are you willing to accept to close a deal or enter a market? Selling abroad will naturally entail more risk than your domestic business. And if things go bad, it's much more difficult to collect.

Some final thoughts to help navigate payment methods and terms:

- **Bad Debt**—Seriously consider adjusting your bad debt reserves to reflect increased activities internationally. Doing so will enable the commercial teams to be a little more aggressive in entering new markets, often a requirement for getting traction. It will also reflect the reality of doing business abroad and avoid financial surprises down the road.

- **Risk**—Similarly, assess terms as a strategic lever to enter a new market. Will taking a little risk on terms, say offering N60 vs. your standard N30, convert potential customers that are currently buying cash in advance from a key competitor? Payment terms are often more important that price, particularly when you factor in lead times for shipping and customs. Distributors/customers overseas may have a hard time justifying buying inventory cash in advance when product might not be available for sale for several months after the initial transaction.

- **Process**—Much of your risk can be mitigated on the front end with a well-defined, methodical, credit review process for new customers. I would highly recommend requiring a site visit as part of this process. One of the only times I've truly been burned was with a "customer" in Uganda who had ordered two containers of product. Our sales lead did all the commercial due diligence needed to "qualify" the customer before passing it over to finance, who made sure all the paperwork was in order and followed up with the required credit references. $100K in initial credit was offered and the order placed. Unfortunately, no one ever actually visited the customer in person—which would have flagged that the entity in question did not actually exist. Once we realized what had happened it was too late, and two containers of product vanished into the ether.

- **Pricing**—With a robust credit review process, one that accounts for the possibility of situations like the one above, actual bad debt can be kept to a minimum. Any bad debt exceeding historical domestic levels can likely be absorbed by minor tweaks in pricing, spreading the cost of a bad customer or two across your entire buyer network.

- **Export Credit Insurance (ECI)**—ECI protects an exporter from risk of non-payment by a foreign buyer. Generally speaking, ECI covers commercial risks (e.g., insolvency of buyer, protracted defaults), as well as political risks (e.g., war, terrorism) that could impact your ability to collect foreign receivables. ECI typically covers ~85-95% with the policy-holder's deductible covering the balance.

ECI is offered by many private insurance companies, but a good place to start here is the Export-Import Bank of the United States (EXIM Bank). On their site, www.exim.gov, you can download their Export Credit Insurance guide, which has a ton of great information on the topic.

CHAPTER TWELVE

# Working with Distributors

Locating the "right" distributor should be the hard part, right? In many cases it is, but a successful distributorship also requires a clear understanding of the relationship, from the perspective of both parties. A written contract is essential, but even during preliminary talks, you should keep in mind some fundamental issues in the manufacturer/distributor relationship:

## DEFINE THE RELATIONSHIP

A critical first question (and one confused enough that it's frequently litigated) is whether you are working with a true distributor, who purchases products and then re-sells them to customers, or with an agent or manufacturer's representative, who never purchases the products outright, but instead, markets them on your behalf. If the relationship being pursued isn't a true distributor situation, the nature of the relationship is fundamentally different; so too should be the contract.

The distinction may also be important in terms of local law, and there are important pros and cons of working with a distributor vs. an agent. For example, the European Agency Directive (EC/86/653) says agents (but not distributors) are entitled to some form of compensation upon the termination of their contract by the principal. The compensation is essentially considered severance if the agent brought you new customers or significantly increased your business with existing customers. Before even beginning to discuss other key terms of your relationship, clarify the exact nature of the relationship and go from there. A basic term sheet can be a helpful tool to help focus the discussion on key points and provide a framework for an eventual definitive agreement.

## DRAFT A SOLID AGREEMENT

There are a lot of free resources/templates online that can serve as a great starting point for thinking about the important issues that should be decided in advance of establishing a formal manufacturer/distributor relationship. A good place to start is the International Chamber of Commerce store at http://store.iccwbo.org/icc-model-contract-on-distributorship which sells the ICC Model Contract on Distributorship, including generally applicable provisions relating to confidentiality, products and territory, advertising, etc. The ICC store also includes free downloads of some standard contract clauses like anti-corruption language, force majeure and hardship clauses and sells other handy, low-cost resources for "going global" businesses, like "Drafting and Negotiating International Commercial Contracts."

But (and it's a big but!), relying strictly on a template agreement is not a good idea for memorializing an international distributorship. Using a "standard form" is particularly problematic because local law varies widely and in ways that are hard to imagine. Take, for example, Puerto Rico, where "Law 21" protects an exclusive sales representative from being terminated by a manufacturer without "just cause." It sounds pretty similar to the EU law above, but Puerto Rico goes a step further with Law 75, which protects a distributor from being terminated by a manufacturer without "just cause." And if you think you can get out of this onerous statute by stating in your agreement that the law of your US state will govern the contract, it won't work. Or bypass the statute by expressly saying in the agreement that the distributorship can be terminated without cause? That won't work either, and the penalties can be severe, including five-year profits and goodwill.

The bottom line: hire a seasoned international business attorney to advise you on the broad strokes of global expansion and find a local attorney to help you navigate local laws. If your domestic attorney doesn't have a good referral, consider starting at the Chambers and Partners website: https://chambers.com/?searchType=name.

It's worth the investment to have a document that is comprehensive in scope, including absolutely essential, non-commercial terms such as, among others, intellectual property, term, termination, liability/warranties, confidentiality, choice of law, and (last but not least) a process for handling disputes. Poorly worded documents drafted by non-lawyers may save you money in the short-term but could ultimately cost much more in terms of time and money fighting over unaddressed issues, or worse yet, potential mediation or litigation on a global scale.

## THINK LONG AND HARD ABOUT EXCLUSIVITY

Exclusivity is a threshold question. With an exclusive distribution agreement, a manufacturer gives a single distributor the sole rights to sell its products in a defined territory. The manufacturer looks for the increased product demand created by a motivated, aggressive seller of its products, while the distributor is free from potential channel competition in "their" territory.

Almost every distributor will ask for exclusivity, but the decision hinges on many factors. Some key questions to think about before coming to any decisions:

- ▶ Will local law permit exclusivity? In the European Union, for example, there are restrictions on exclusivity.
- ▶ What does exclusivity mean—can the manufacturer itself sell directly in the exclusive territory (e.g., direct to an OEM), or are other distributors the only parties banned from selling?
- ▶ Is exclusivity defined by territory, vertical, channel, product, or some combination of these (and potentially other) factors?
- ▶ What about sales to a customer in one territory resulting in a drop shipment to the customer's branch office in another distributor's exclusive territory?

- Should any of the manufacturer's existing accounts be excluded?
- Is the distributor allowed to sell to sub-agents or sub-distributors?
- Is the exclusivity mutual (is the distributor allowed to sell your competitor's product within the territory)?
- What is required for the distributor to maintain exclusivity—is it a "good faith" effort to sell the product or (more frequently) are there minimum purchase provisions? Are those minimum purchase provisions enforceable?
- Do you understand the antitrust and non-competition rules relating to the granting of exclusivity? What implications are there for price? Here again, consultation with a local attorney is essential.
- If exclusivity is terminated, is the whole agreement considered terminated?
- What about "new products"—will those be excluded from exclusivity but an "updated product" remains subject to exclusivity provision? How are those terms defined to minimize misunderstanding?
- What are the consequences of terminating the exclusivity (see below)?

Keep in mind there are alternatives to granting a distributor exclusive rights to sell your product in a designated geography. These alternatives may satisfy everyone's key objectives without triggering the extra risks—legal and otherwise—associated with exclusivity. A few alternatives to exclusivity include:

- **Assigning Areas of Primary Responsibility ("APRs"):** An APR clause requires a distributor to use its "best efforts" or "reasonable efforts" to sell a manufacturer's product in a particular area, but doesn't preclude the distributor from selling outside of the APR. Performance goals can be set to clarify the goal within the APR. Keep in mind that APRs of different distributors can overlap, either in the initial contract or later if one distributor fails to meet its performance targets.

- **Drop-Shipments:** For a specified fee, a manufacturer may elect to ship products directly to the distributor's customer, saving the distributor the cost of storage, handling, and reshipment. A common structure is to have manufacturers agree to drop-ship only to customers located within a distributor's APR.

- **Location Clauses:** A location clause specifies that a distributor can only receive product shipments at designed warehouses or facilities. This may encourage distributors to sell within a specific area.

- **Pass-Over Clauses:** Pass-over clauses say that if a distributor sells outside of its APR, it must pay the distributor located within that APR a portion of the purchase price.

## DON'T NEGLECT TERMINATION

Many parties don't want to even *consider* the possibility that a newly established relationship won't be successful, or that it will likely run its course after a fixed period of time. But failing to plan for termination can do significant damage down the road.

Key considerations when negotiating termination rights include:

- Should termination be allowed (with notice) for any reason or only for "cause"? How is cause defined? Keep in mind that some jurisdictions have specific statutes providing additional legal protection for certain types of businesses upon termination, and others, like Brazil, may require a court order to terminate.
- Is the termination right mutual?
- Once terminated, what happens to inventory? Accounts receivable? IP? Product registrations/compliance programs the distributor might have previously handled? Customer lists?
- What are the financial consequences of terminating? Remember that in some countries, "goodwill payments" are required upon termination, regardless of what the contract actually says and what "choice of law" you've decided will govern the agreement. Puerto Rico's Rule 75 was mentioned above, but other jurisdictions have similar legislation, such as Spain and Germany.
- Is a terminated distributor required to cooperate with an on-boarding distributor?

Finally, be sure to include in any termination provision which clauses of the agreement "survive" termination. For example, consider the scenario where a distributor holds trade secrets of the manufacturer. Without a continuing confidentiality provision, the distributor may be able to exploit those trade secrets post-termination.

## COVER ALL YOUR BASES

Here, the devil's in the details. Rather than being viewed as a legal necessity, the distribution agreement should be viewed as a critical document outlining key commercial terms and relative expectations. Laying out the fundamental business terms that define your relationship—which can and should be done in plain language—will get the relationship off on the right foot and likely save you an extraordinary amount of time and headache down the road. Many otherwise healthy seller-buyer relationships inadvertently went south because the parties simply didn't anticipate, discuss, and contract for key issues.

### Essential Commercial Terms

Each situation will be unique but here is a (non-exhaustive) list of essential commercial terms and questions for consideration:

- **Pricing**: A key commercial term, obviously. Ensure you address as many potential questions as possible, including:
  - What is the initial pricing; when and how will pricing adjustments occur?
  - How much notice must be provided for adjustments?
  - Does pricing include taxes and customs duties?
  - In what currency will pricing be quoted?
  - How will currency fluctuations be handled?

▷ How and when will adjustments be made if a product is heavily dependent on the price of raw materials that fluctuate? i.e., is there a set formula based on a commodity index?

▷ Will you offer the distributor volume discounts or other special pricing program dependent on meeting certain performance targets?

► **Payments**: As mentioned earlier, payment terms are a key commercial decision. Make sure it's agreed to and spelled out in detail in the agreement.

▷ On what terms will you sell to the distributor?

▷ Method of payment—cash in advance, letter of credit, bill of exchange? Open account? Security and guarantees of payment? Currency used?

▷ How will late payments be handled?

► **Territory**: For obvious reasons, be as precise as possible in defining the geographic territory associated with the distributorship.

► **Logistics**: Use Incoterms, discussed in detail in Chapter 11, to define relative logistics obligations between you and your buyer.

► **Product Labeling, Testing, Packaging, Inspection:**

▷ Who is responsible for the above and what approvals are required?

- ▷ Will cancellations or returns be accepted and on what basis?
- ▷ Required language(s)?

- ▶ **Performance Requirements:**
  - ▷ What are sales quotas and/or performance targets and what are the consequences for not meeting them?
  - ▷ Will product mix be considered in performance targets, or only aggregate sales volume?
  - ▷ When will performance targets be adjusted and under what circumstances?
  - ▷ Will a "rolling" system be used for purposes of tracking performance targets?
  - ▷ What methodology will be used for tracking?
  - ▷ Are there audit rights?

- ▶ **Marketing:**
  - ▷ Who will create localized marketing materials? If distributor is responsible for materials, manufacturer should maintain a right to review marketing materials (subject to a notice period) or, at minimum, a veto.
  - ▷ Who will pay for local programs? Are market development funds available, and if so, based on what criteria?
  - ▷ How will new product launches be handled?
  - ▷ Who is responsible for translation of marketing materials?

- **Business Planning:**
  - What is the initial inventory investment required, and minimum levels ongoing?
  - How many salespeople will be dedicated to selling your products? What kind of skill sets do they need? Will the headcount be keyed to the level of sales (i.e., a certain ratio to volume)?

- **Forecasting & Demand Planning:**
  - How frequently will a distributor be required to forecast and for what period of time?
  - How will adjustments to forecasts be handled and what are the consequences of not adhering to agreed-upon processes?
  - What obligation does manufacturer have to inform distributor of supply issues and how are backorders prioritized?

- **Post-Sales Support:**
  - What warranty is offered? Are there limitations to that warranty (be aware of destination country requirements around minimum warranty coverage!)?
  - How will returns/repairs be handled?
  - Who provides after-sales support functions?
  - What training does distributor receive (and from whom) regarding after-sales support? What are your expectations regarding after-sales support in terms of headcount and responsiveness to customers?

As business people eager to get a commercial relationship up and running, we tend to shy away from the heavy lifting required to negotiate potentially contentious terms. We don't want to slow things down, have "uncomfortable" discussions with new customers, or sit for too long in the same room as an attorney. But in the end, it's worth it. Take the time and make the investment to have really good buyer-seller agreements that are localized to the market in which you're doing business. Not only will you minimize risk and avoid potential legal issues down the road, but from a commercial standpoint, you will set a great foundation for a long-term relationship by clearly defining roles and responsibilities, setting expectations (on both sides), and establishing a focal point for future discussions as the partnership develops over time.

CHAPTER THIRTEEN

# Managing Risk

As we discussed earlier, doing business overseas can be risky in a variety of ways. In this chapter, we'll take a deeper dive into two areas that should be top priority for almost every business: Corruption and IP.

## CORRUPTION

Whether yours is a small company with five employees or a multinational enterprise with five thousand, every US company doing *any* business outside the US has to think about the risks associated with corruption. There are many laws covering anti-bribery and corrupt practices, but the largest and most well-known US law is the Foreign Corrupt Practices Act (FCPA).

For companies not required to submit reports to the SEC under the Exchange Act, the most relevant provisions of the FCPA are the anti-bribery provisions, which essentially make it a crime for any US person, business or employee to offer/provide (directly **or** through a third party) anything of value to a foreign government official with intent to influence or to gain an unfair advantage. You probably noticed the word "intent"—be aware that the standard is quite low. Intent/knowledge is usually inferred from the fact that the bribery took place and cases have shown that "willful blindness" may well put violators in prison.

## Is Corruption Really that Common?

Although the US is certainly not immune to corruption in business, the relative ethics of American businesses compared to operating practice in many countries sometimes creates a blind spot for US companies expanding abroad. Some may assume that unless a business is corrupt at the highest levels, there's no risk of corruption in the rank and file, among salespeople in the field, or distributors in a region. Conversely, executives in the home office who are themselves highly ethical may not always understand the nuts and bolts of how business is being transacted internationally.

But corruption and bribery in the international context is significant. Consider the following:

- ▶ Nearly half of workers across Europe, the Middle East, Africa and India think bribery and corruption are acceptable ways to survive an economic downturn. *(Source: Ernst and Young,* 'Navigating today's complex business risks Europe Middle East, India and Africa Fraud Survey')

- Around the world nearly one in four said that they paid a bribe when accessing public services in the last 12 months (*Source: Transparency International*).
- Thirty percent of respondents to a corruption survey said they believed they have lost major deals to corrupt competitors (*Source: Control Risks, International Business Attitudes to Corruption Survey*)

Simply put, international business corruption—bribes, kickbacks, false and unrecorded transactions—is common but frequently ignored for many reasons. Exacerbating the risk to smaller US companies doing business overseas is a lack of cultural context, language differences, and absence of a seasoned legal team who can help navigate the landmines surrounding the reality of international corruption.

For more detailed information on how corruption impacts various regions/countries around the world, check out the following link: https://www.transparency.org/news/feature/global_corruption_barometer_citizens_voices_from_around_the_world

## Is the FCPA Actually Enforced?

In a word, yes. The FCPA was enacted in 1977 and enforcement was quite low for almost 25 years. Since 2005, however, it's picked up significantly and continues to increase each year. The Department of Justice, SEC, and FBI all have units dedicated to investigation and prosecution, and several agencies have staff in key overseas markets for just this purpose. In fact, 2019 was a high-water mark in terms of FCPA actions with more than $2.6

billion in corporate fines. The chart below from Stanford Law School highlights the point.

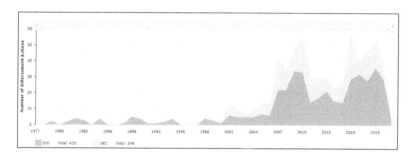

**Chart:** *Number of FCPA enforcement actions by year*

Both companies and managers/employees can be prosecuted under the FCPA. So this isn't just an issue for your company—it could be an issue for you personally.

## How Can I Minimize My Company's Risk?

1. **Fully Assess the Risk**

   ▶ **By Geography**—Naturally, the first step in assessing your company's risk is to focus on those countries in which you're currently doing business as well as those you envision entering in the near future. One easy user-friendly resource is transparency.org (link above) which compiles a Corruption Perceptions Index. The index ranks 180 countries and territories on a 0 to 100 point scale (corrupt to clean) by their perceived levels of public sector corruption according to experts and businesspeople. In 2020, the index found that more than two-thirds of countries score below 50, with an average score of 43 (for reference, the US score in 2020 was 67, while the US's two largest trading partners scored at 77 (Canada) and 31 (Mexico). The region with the highest average score was Western Europe (average score of 66) while sub-Saharan Africa (average score of 32), Eastern Europe, and Central Asia (average score of 34) had the largest amount of perceived corruption. If you're thinking of expanding to one of the popular BRICI countries, note that in 2020 these countries scored as follows: Brazil (38), Russia (30), India (40), China (42) and Indonesia (37).

▶ **By Business Structure**—Equally important is to ask some critical questions about how your business is structured and how much interaction your company (or its agents) has with government officials. "Government official" is defined broadly under the FCPA, including low level employees of government-owned companies. In many countries, healthcare and education are government run, meaning that doctors, professors, and a variety of other professionals are deemed "government officials" for purposes of the FCPA. So consider:

▷ What kind of business does your company do outside the US?

▷ How much government involvement is required—for example, do you need permits and/or does your business need to qualify products for sale?

▷ Do you use agents, distributors, and intermediaries in the course of your foreign business? The FCPA defines "intermediary" as a third party who assists the company in some aspect of its local business activity. The government assumes you have independently confirmed that your intermediaries are not involved in corruption, so don't expect (as many do) to hide behind a shield of an intermediary. Ninety percent of FCPA cases involve conduct by third parties, so make sure you understand how many intermediaries you have and what (if any) relationship they have to government officials of any kind. When dealing with third parties, be particularly wary of intermediaries who are government employees (or who have close relatives in government positions), excessive commissions, large discounts to distributors, consultant agreements with vague services, shell companies and payment to offshore accounts.

▷ Are you involved in litigation in overseas markets? The judicial process necessarily involves court officials and judges that are routinely bribed in some foreign markets.

▷ How is shipping structured—do you use freight forwarders and customs agents?

▷ Are "facilitation payments" common practice in your target geography or industry sector? Facilitation payments are small bribes made to induce routine functions they are otherwise obligated to perform. Unlike a bribe, these are not payments made directly to obtain or retain business. An example of a facilitation payment would be a small payment to ensure scheduling of inspections associated with transit of goods across a country. It's important to note that while the FCPA contains a narrow exception for "facilitating or expediting payments" made in routine, non-discretionary governmental actions, it's a gray area that can get you into trouble if not clearly understood and managed with internal controls and compliance procedures.

2. **Establish a Compliance Program (even if basic)**

   ▶ **Insist on FCPA Language in Every Foreign Contract**—Simply put, have a lawyer draft a basic provision relating to FCPA that is non-negotiable with potential partners. It should, at a minimum, provide that the partner 1) understands and will comply with the FCPA, 2) assists with any investigation that arises from a FCPA claim, and 3) agrees that you may terminate the contract immediately upon any violation. A well-written FCPA provision is a no-brainer as a first step in mitigating your risk under FCPA.

   ▶ **Assign Ownership**—A standalone FCPA Compliance Policy is fairly straightforward to develop and administer and various online sources have checklists and guidance on best practices. Do not assume that a small amount of language about international corruption buried in your Standards of Business Conduct will do, as history has shown it clearly will not. The agencies enforcing FCPA rely heavily on showings of "good faith" in a company's compliance efforts, which require that a member of senior management be designated a responsible party and be accountable for the program.

- **Train Management, Employees, and Third Parties**—If you have the budget (particularly if you're in a high-risk category for purposes of the FCPA), hire a skilled in-person trainer to educate senior management and business leaders, and in an ideal world, all parties who could expose you to liability under FCPA. A personalized trainer will enable your managers and employees to familiarize themselves with the actual corruption risks in your industry, the countries where you do business, and with the specific business model your company is employing. In-person training is certainly preferable to other options, although many online resources have developed basic training programs for employees and related parties for even the smallest of businesses.

- **Establish Internal Controls over Finances**—First, understand there is not a concept of "materiality" in the FCPA, which means that the government doesn't care if a bribe is small or big. Make sure your company is keeping books/records which accurately document all transactions and which flag ones that are potentially fictional and/or corrupt. Additionally, have someone familiar with FCPA watch over internal financial controls.

- **Don't Rely too Heavily on the "Facilitating Payments" Loophole**—The FCPA includes a provision allowing that "any facilitating or expediting payment to a foreign official . . . the purpose of which is to expedite or to secure the performance of a routine governmental action by a foreign official" is a permissible payment. This may sound broad, but be aware that *facilitating payments* originated as an extremely narrow exception, and according to some legal experts, will in fact become obsolete over time. Making reliance on the loophole even trickier is the fact that little interpretative guidance exists as to when it can be lawfully used (and even if a payment doesn't violate FCPA, it may still violate other anti-corruption laws and/or local laws in the country you're doing business). Before considering whether to use the loophole, acquaint yourself with the detailed requirements and be aware that any payments need to be well documented.

Establishing relationships that enable your company's goods to cross the ocean may seem overwhelming enough, and the legalese of corruption compliance may seem out of reach. Due to the risk involved, however, it's a critical piece of your international expansion strategy. A good place to start is the FCPA Resource Guide published by the Department of Justice and SEC: https://www.justice.gov/criminal-fraud/fcpa-resource-guide. In it, you'll find "real life" hypotheticals that may answer your particular questions.

## PROTECTING A US COMPANY'S IP OVERSEAS

In 2001, Jim O'Neill, a well-reputed British economist, coined the term BRIC by suggesting that the four countries—Brazil, Russia, India and China—have the potential to be economic giants by 2050. More recently, US businesses have added Indonesia to the "BRIC" convention as a location with (potentially) abundant opportunity for US companies expanding abroad: BRICI. Over the last two decades, however, US companies have learned the hard way that those same countries share another key attribute—

they are among the riskiest on the planet in terms of intellectual property protection. With a growing number of US business going global every year, especially to BRICI countries, it is imperative to think about safeguarding your intellectual property even in the early days of the planning process.

In the US, the procedure for protecting intellectual property is unambiguous: register your trademark or copyright or file a patent or provisional patent application with US Patent and Trademark Office. Many, unfortunately, assume that IP protection in the US extends globally. It most definitely does not. The extent of your exposure really depends on the law of the countries in which you're doing business, and that, in and of itself, gets very complicated.

The best way to protect your IP during international expansion is to have legal counsel develop a global IP policy, working with local agents to execute that strategy in various markets. IP laws are very technical, regionally distinct, and compliance can be a nightmare for a layperson: outsourcing is almost always the best way to go given what's at stake. Just make sure you're outsourcing wisely. Ask for referrals from people who know what they're doing. Research agents' credibility and read reviews. Make sure you sign a contract that is not only explicit about what will be done, but that is enforceable in both the home country and the target country. More generally speaking, here are five key steps to getting off on the right foot when it comes to protecting IP overseas:

## STEP 1: Understand Your Risks

The initial question: where do you want to expand and how much exposure to IP infringement do you have in those markets? The internet is swimming with information on which countries are most and least protective of IP, so do your research to evaluate the risks to your business, and weigh that against the potential upside of expansion. For example, the International Property Rights Index (found here: https://www.internationalpropertyrightsindex.org/countries) publishes an annual global scorecard for IP protection. No BRICI countries ranked "better" than #59 (out of 125) in its 2018 rankings: Brazil #55, Russia #84, India #59, China #52, and Indonesia #64. Who claims the top spots, you might wonder? (In order of rank): Finland, New Zealand, Switzerland, Norway, Singapore, Sweden, Australia, the Netherlands, Luxembourg, Canada, Japan, Denmark, the UK and . . . at #14, the United States.

## STEP 2: Streamline (if possible)

Rather than painstakingly following law country by country, you may be able to protect your IP through one of the treaty frameworks like the following:

- ▶ **PCT**—The International Patent System: The Patent Cooperation Treaty (PCT) assists applicants in seeking patent protection internationally for their inventions and facilitates public access to a wealth of technical information relating to those inventions. By filing one international patent application under the PCT, applicants can simultaneously seek protection for an invention in over 150 countries, including the BRICI countries (minus Russia).

- **Madrid**—The International Trademark System: The Madrid System is a convenient and cost-effective solution for registering and managing trademarks worldwide. File a single application and pay one set of fees to apply for protection in ~190 countries. Through the Madrid System, you can modify, renew, or expand your global trademark portfolio through one centralized system.

- **Hague**—The International Design System: The Hague System for the International Registration of Industrial Designs provides a practical business solution for registering up to 100 designs through filing a single international application. Geographic application is limited, however, and excludes most BRICI countries.

- **Berne Convention for the Protection of Literary and Artistic Works**—The Berne Convention covers copyrights and extends some copyright protection to 176 "contracting parties," including all BRICI countries.

## STEP 3: Use Resources to Understand Country-by-Country Protection (if no treaty is available)

Patents and trademarks are territorial and must be filed in each country where protection is sought. For more information on how to apply for individual patents or trademarks in a foreign country, contact the intellectual property office in that country directly. A list of contact information for most intellectual property offices worldwide can be found on the Intellectual Property Organization portal at https://www.wipo.int/portal/en/index.html.

Each country has its local norms and rules as well, and those rules may have serious implications for your business. In China, for example, trademarks are granted on a "first to file" basis, meaning the first to file a trademark application automatically owns the mark, regardless of who developed or first used the mark. This can result in "trademark squatting," where due to the "first to file" trademark system, someone can apply opportunistically for a trademark with the intent to sell the mark back to its original creator. The best way to prevent trademark squatting is to register your trademark—in English and Chinese or its local versions—before anyone else. If there's a remote chance you might do business in China someday, for example, act sooner rather than later.

Even if you hire an expert to navigate the process, you should make use of publicly available resources to educate yourself on the basics so you can feel comfortable your interests are being protected. The site www.StopFakes.gov includes intellectual property rights toolkits that provide detailed information about protecting and enforcing intellectual property rights in specific markets, along with contact information for local intellectual property rights offices abroad and US government officials available to assist you. US embassies in the following locations have posted IP toolkits designed to help US companies seeking IP protection overseas:

- Brazil
- Brunei
- Colombia
- Egypt

- European Union
- Italy
- Korea
- Malaysia
- Peru
- Singapore
- Thailand
- Vietnam

Similarly, the UK Intellectual Property Office (IPO) (found here: https://www.gov.uk/government/organisations/intellectual-property-office) has produced a range of country-specific guides to help you protect and manage your IP abroad. These guides describe the issues you may face with IP infringement, how to deal with them, and where to find sources of further help. Available country guides include:

- Brazil
- China
- India
- Korea
- South Africa
- Turkey
- US
- Vietnam

Also consider whether there is regional protection available, which could ease the burden of filing for IP protection in multiple jurisdictions.

## STEP 4: Research Potential Partners, Watch Your Contracts, and Beef Up Your Security

Central to protecting your IP overseas is requiring that local manufacturers or potential business partners sign a non-disclosure agreement specifically designed for the local market. These contracts may be written in the local language, but make sure the contract can be enforced by local laws. In addition, it's critical that you develop detailed IP language for licensing and subcontracting contracts in local markets.

As a matter of practice, conduct thorough due diligence of potential foreign partners, including background checks, to make sure you're avoiding players likely to exploit your IP. The US Commercial Service (www.export.gov) can be very helpful on this front.

In addition to vetting potential partners and protecting yourself contractually, consider augmenting your security procedures by:

- ▶ Limiting IP access to carefully selected parties
- ▶ Physically locking areas where IP is stored
- ▶ Prohibiting unauthorized copies of IP, such as on USB devices, shared network drives
- ▶ Encrypting IP transmitted digitally and electronically

- Ensuring sensitive information is kept on password-protected areas of your system
- Installing anti-virus software and keeping it up to date
- Installing firewalls to prevent unauthorized users from hacking into your system
- Backing up your work and ensuring back-ups are stored securely, preferably off site
- Protecting your system against power surges and failures

## STEP 5: Monitor the Market for Infringements

Once your IP rights have been secured in key markets, monitor the market for infringements. For example, most Chinese e-commerce sites have takedown procedures that allow IP rights owners to apply to have IP-infringing product listings removed. If you are particularly concerned with infringing products, register your IP with China Customs. Most IP seizures made by China Customs are trademark infringing goods being exported from China.

Along those same lines, register your IP with US Customs and Border Protection (CBP) via an Intellectual Property Rights e-Recordation (IPRR) application, available online at https://iprr.cbp.gov/. As an intellectual property right owner, you can partner with CBP to help protect your registered and recorded rights. CBP can detain and seize imported goods that violate intellectual property rights in the United States. To learn more, read *How to Work with CBP to Protect Your Intellectual Property*, found here: https://www.cbp.gov/document/publications/work-cbp-protect-your-intellectual-property-rights.

Particularly in high-risk situations, consider acquiring IP insurance that protects against the potentially significant legal costs of IP violations. Policies vary and can be quite costly, but an IP insurance policy may cover both the enforcement and defense of claims. Remedies may include damages, such as loss of profits or reputation and settlements to any IP right domestically or internationally.

The bottom line is this: your IP is your most valuable asset. Protect it accordingly.

CHAPTER FOURTEEN

# International Growth Drivers

As we've been discussing throughout, winning in the international arena is tough; there are simply no shortcuts. Success requires good strategy, thoughtful planning, adept execution, perseverance, tolerance for risk, and some good old-fashioned luck. While the tendency is to focus on "big" issues to drive growth—product positioning, pricing, business development, partnerships—many more fly under the radar, but can potentially be equally as impactful.

As some final food for thought, I'd like to leave you with a summary of some tactical tweaks you can make to accelerate and optimize your international expansion plans. We've discussed some of these topics in detail, but I'd suggest using this as an actionable checklist to ensure you're not overlooking some quick wins that might be right in front of you:

# MARKET DEVELOPMENT FUND (MDF) PROGRAMS

Allocating a portion of your marketing budget to in-country channel partners for local program management can be a very effective use of marketing dollars in several ways. If you're in business with the right partner (distributor, retailer, etc.) they should be in a better position than headquarter marketing to determine the best use of small, tactical budgets, including localized messaging, optimal platforms, and the general tone of marketing activities. Tying these dollars to specific performance metrics (e.g., percent of sales, minimum volume requirements, etc.) can have the added benefit of incentivizing behaviors in line with your commercial objectives. MDF programs should be developed with strategic rigor and detailed policies and procedures, but there are some universal best practice considerations around key program steps:

- **MDF Request**—Design an MDF request form or process to help guide the partner in using the right tactics and marketing assets along with specific objectives in terms of customer conversion, incremental revenue, etc.

- **Review and Approval**—Select programs for investments based on specific return on investment metrics and strategic objectives; place your bets accordingly vs. taking shotgun approach

- **Execution**—Employ centralized tools and templates, program management, oversight, and work process reporting procedures; facilitate knowledge sharing and best practices across geographies

► **Review**—Require partners to report results, validate return on investment; incorporate results into a dashboard with key metrics for partner review and comparison across partner geographies for future investment decisions

## DISTRIBUTION AGREEMENTS

As we discussed in Chapter 12, distribution/channel partner agreements are a sound practice in any international business setting. While often under the purview of the legal department with a focus on key tactical elements (risk mitigation, warranty expectations, geographic coverage, etc.), agreements can also serve as an extremely effective platform to support key growth-oriented goals for the business.

► **Partner Requirements**—Clearly and specifically defining "distributor requirements" in detail from a commercial perspective—minimum inventory levels, number of dedicated sales resources, annual marketing spend—can set the right expectations up front and avoid conflict down the road

► **Term**—Make periodic renewals dependent on meeting specific annual sales objectives that are agreed to at the beginning of the year; it doesn't mean you will terminate if the partner falls short, but it should provide the right focus and incentive to work toward common objectives

> ► **Reporting**—Use the agreement to define up-front what information you need and to ensure your partner understands what's expected (e.g., monthly sales forecasts, marketing expenditure); again, setting the expectation in advance and getting it in writing will be much more effective than ad hoc report requests once the relationship is up and running

Every business will have a unique set of commercial drivers, but the point here is to view the distribution agreement as more than just a legal document that defines and sets expectations around key commercial activities. You will rarely have more leverage than this point in the relationship, so lock in what you need now.

## CREDIT TERMS/LIMITS

Growing internationally will almost certainly increase the risk profile of your business, with collection risk being just one obvious example. Instead of taking an overly conservative approach, which is the natural inclination, view this as an opportunity to potentially differentiate from domestic competitors you are confronting overseas (who likely share your same concerns around risk). Everything else being equal, offering more attractive terms than your competitor can be a major factor in converting customers, particularly in overseas markets. This may be uncomfortable initially, but here are a few considerations to mitigate risk:

> ► **Customer Validation**—Do your diligence on new customers. Credit references, banking information, trade references are helpful, but someone from your organization needs to go there and see the business for yourself.

- **Credit Vehicles**—Consider documentary collection as a way to provide ample credit while reducing risk. Somewhere between open credit and a letter of credit in terms of risk and complexity, a documentary collections transaction takes place between banks after goods are shipped but before the importer takes ownership.

- **Increasing Bad Debt Reserves**—Your CFO will likely be uncomfortable here, but budgeting for some increased risk can be a good way to manage everyone's expectations about the benefits, and potential costs, of being more aggressive with international credit terms. A good way to offset the added potential cost here is with modest price increases for international customers.

## SALES INCENTIVES

This may seem like an obvious one, but I've seen a lot of organizations where incentives for sales leaders, as well as more junior "feet on the street," are misaligned with the company's objectives for international growth (or they just mirror domestic programs). If the current goal is market penetration in new geographies, for example, incentives should likely center around customer conversion. To take growth to the next level, volume or revenue should likely come into play. And as momentum slows with higher levels of penetration, transitioning to more profitable mix, or incremental sales growth will likely be more important than overall volume. In any case, I'm a firm believer that incentive programs should adhere to some key principles and guidelines:

- Qualitative objectives should play a very minor role in the bonus formula (if at all!); bonus criteria should be specific and measurable
- Senior sales leaders should have some allocation for overall company targets, e.g., company EBITDA, so they "have some skin in the game" in terms of overall company performance
- Sales bonuses should be paid on a relatively frequent basis so that incentives are tied to the actual results you're trying to encourage

## VOLUME REBATES

Discounts and rebates are often a point of contention between the commercial and financial camps in the business. The finance group is not always wrong. Too often discounts and rebates spin out of control and end up being a margin giveaway without a corresponding benefit to the business. If structured strategically, however, discounts and rebates can be an effective tool to help drive growth in target markets. Consider:

- Allocating a discretionary budget to salespeople for spot trading to help drive volume
- Providing year-end volume rebates for customers in key regions based on incremental growth over prior year
- Implementing pricing levels with tiered discounts off price list based on order size or periodic volume targets

## PROJECT FUNDING

Hundreds to thousands of NGOs and government agencies around the globe provide financing and other support for projects to promote a particular mission—e.g., sustainable energy in Africa, economic development in priority countries, export facilitation for domestic companies. Working with and through the right organization can support ongoing business development efforts and open the door into otherwise difficult to penetrate markets. The most relevant entity for your business to reach out to will depend on your particular market segment and target geography, but here are a few examples of US government entities that offer trade financing instruments to help exporters expand into new markets (and are a good place to start):

- ► The Export-Import Bank of the United States (EXIM)—offers credit, finance, and insurance products to US exporters
- ► The Overseas Private Investment Corporation (OPIC)—offers loans, guarantees, and political risk insurance
- ► The US Trade and Development Agency—facilitates participation of US businesses in host country priority development projects
- ► The Millennium Challenge Corporation—offers project assistance grants to countries committed to sustainable local economic development and good governance

# IP PROTECTION RIGHTS (IPR)

Although exact figures are hard to determine, a private watchdog group recently estimated that counterfeits cost the US economy between $225 billion and $600 billion per year. A lot of this is unavoidable—it's the nature of the world today—but developing and implementing a fundamentally sound IP protection program can go a long way toward ensuring sales of your products and services go to your company, and not a local counterfeiter. Working with experienced legal counsel to develop an overall IPR protection strategy is a must, but here are some basic, low-cost steps just about every business should consider early on:

- ▶ Develop detailed IPR language in licensing, subcontracting, and distribution agreements
- ▶ Conduct sufficient due diligence on potential foreign partners (US Commercial Services International Partner Search is a great resource)
- ▶ Record US-registered trademarks and copyrights with Customs and Border Protection
- ▶ Secure and register patents, trademarks, and copyrights in key foreign markets, including defensively in particularly high-risk countries where you don't yet have a local presence

## COMMUNICATION AND COLLABORATION TOOLS

Anyone who's worked for a domestic US company overseas will tell you one of the greatest challenges is daily communication with the mother ship. Not only are there logistical challenges such as time zone differences, but doing most of your communication via email or phone can have a significant impact on productivity and effectiveness—one that amplifies over time. Customers are in the same boat, and almost always complain of too little (vs. too much) communication from US headquarters. There is no replacement for sitting face-to-face across a conference room table, but implementing a thoughtful plan here can improve the bottom line by responding to opportunities and challenges in a more proactive, efficient, and effective manner. Here are some effective tools to get the ball rolling:

- **Videoconferencing**—Use video not just for one-on-one calls (Skype) but for working sessions between HQ and field teams (and customers) via Zoom, Teams, or some other platform. Even though many are experiencing Zoom burn-out during the COVID-19 pandemic, relative to non-video phone calls you'll experience increased engagement, improved team dynamics, and facilitate buy-in from all parties.

- **CRM**—Customer Relationship Management tools like Salesforce.com can be a very effective way to automate and streamline key processes, workflows, approvals, as well as facilitate collaboration around commercial opportunities.

- **Social Media**—A robust social media strategy should incorporate participation from internal constituents as well. For example, an internal Facebook page where employees in the field can post customer comments or pictures of completed projects can go a long way toward building excitement and facilitating communication and collaboration with those out in the marketplace.

## TECHNICAL TRAINING

Again, hard to quantify but technical product training can have a meaningful and lasting impact on the bottom line of your business. Engaging overseas partners in organized training sessions (ideally in person) generates enthusiasm for your products and services and can give channel partners tangible tools to outsell your competition. Similarly, employees who have been properly trained on your offering can address questions and troubleshoot in a more proactive and efficient manner. A customer service rep who can answer a technical question without having to involve an engineer, for example, will feel more empowered and the engineer can continue to focus on more value-added activities without distraction. Most importantly, the customer issue is addressed sooner rather than later, and can go about the business of using, selling, or promoting your products.

As mentioned up front, this is not an exhaustive list, and not one of these drivers alone is likely to be a game-changer for your organization (although you never know!). Aggregated, however, they are "doable" relative to major strategic initiatives, and can have a significant impact on the commercial objectives of your international business. If each of the drivers above contributes just an incremental 1-2% in growth per year, the business will grow at additional 10-15% per year. That's great payback.

APPENDIX A:

# Checklist of Key Requirements

The planning checklist below can serve as a starting point for assessing your readiness (or current capability) to compete abroad. My recommendation would be to define the 20–30 key requirements for success of *your particular business*, take a good look in the mirror to identify gaps, and put in place an action plan to address these deficiencies. This effort will yield massive returns as you move from planning to execution.

# CHECKLIST OF KEY REQUIREMENTS | 159

| Driver* | | | Objective | Readiness (1-5) |
|---|---|---|---|---|
| 1 | STRATEGIC | Strategic Objectives | Clearly defined and measurable objectives that support the strategic priorities of the company for international growth, with buy-in across the management team, shareholders, and other key constituents | |
| 2 | | Target Geographies | Prioritized short list of target geographies based on methodical weighting and scoring of key market attractiveness and accessibility criteria | |
| 3 | | Target Verticals | Prioritized list of targets applications/verticals leveraging core business in domestic markets and/or existing customer and channel relationships | |
| 4 | | Competitive Positioning | Clearly delineated differentiation vis-à-vis the international competitive set and thorough understanding of local KPIs including trade-offs between price, quality, and value | |
| 5 | | Landed Cost Modeling | Thorough understanding of landed cost to inform pricing, determine actual gross margins, and identify areas along the value chain to improve service and/or profitability | |
| 6 | COMMERCIAL | Currency | Strategic approach to billing/AR that accounts for exchange rate risk, customer expectations, and administrative complexity (e.g., billing in local currency or $USD) | |
| 7 | | Pricing | Systematic approach to pricing that drives strategic objectives (e.g., share vs. margin), aligns internal objectives (e.g., finance vs. sales), and clearly defines key processes including adjustments, discounts, rebates, and adjustment timing/methodology | |
| 8 | | Distribution Agreements | Distribution/customer agreements that address requirements unique to the international business, e.g., goodwill indemnity, warranty, implied exclusivity, etc. | |
| 9 | | Credit Terms | Country-specific terms that account for local competitive dynamics and operational realities, including time lag between shipment of goods and clearing of customs in local market | |
| 10 | | Collaboration Tools | Dynamic set of digital communication, document sharing, and project management tools to streamline communication among HQ, field resources, customers, suppliers, and other constituents | |

| Driver* | | Objective | Readiness (1-5) |
|---|---|---|---|
| 11 | OPERATIONAL | Local Product Requirements — Product designed and developed to meet local product requirements, balancing global scale and efficiency with local KPCs | |
| 12 | | Incoterms — Strategic use of incoterms that incorporates trade-offs between risk, cost, customer experience, and potential treatment of freight as a profit center | |
| 13 | | Forecasting/S&OP — Dynamic, disciplined process with sales, operations, and finance, balancing customer needs with financial and operational drivers of the business | |
| 14 | | Freight Management — Treatment of freight and logistics management as a competitor differentiator, with focus on key customer satisfaction metrics including on-time delivery, cost efficiency, competitive lead times, and minimal damaged goods claims | |
| 15 | | Structure/Entity Selection — International entity structure that balances long-term strategic plan for the business with the pragmatic realities of gaining traction and managing the business in short/medium term | |
| 16 | ADMINISTRATIVE | Credit Policy/Approvals — Clearly defined and articulated process for reviewing new credit applications and existing customer credit levels based on strategic balance between bad debt reserves and need to drive new business | |
| 17 | | Payroll Management — Payroll management system that balances cost with ability to scale with growth in the organization while meeting local payroll requirements (third party) | |
| 18 | | Reporting Matrix — Detailed map of relative roles and responsibilities for supporting international business requirements, with clearly articulated solid and dotted reporting lines across and within various business functions | |
| 19 | | Management Capability — Sufficient international business capabilities within the management team to meet initial objectives as well as support growth and added complexity in the business over time | |
| 20 | | Customer Onboarding — Detailed process for customer onboarding including initial screening, credit checks, credit approvals, contracting, order submission, training, digital asset management, and AR policies | |

## CHECKLIST OF KEY REQUIREMENTS | 161

| Driver* | | Objective | Readiness (1-5) |
|---|---|---|---|
| 21 | RISK | IP Protection | Proactive implementation of systemic IP protection plan in current and <u>potential</u> markets, including trademarks, patents, copyrights, domain names, trade secrets, and trade dress | |
| 22 | | FCPA/UK Anti-Bribery | A comprehensive and dynamic FCPA training and compliance program covering onboarding and continuing education at all levels within the organization, as well as with relevant third parties | |
| 23 | | Data Protection/ Privacy | Comprehensive data security regime that complies with local jurisdictions including GDPR (Europe), UK Data Protection, and PIPEDA (Canada) | |
| 24 | | Warranty Policy | Clearly defined and articulated, country-specific warranty policies that balances minimum local legal requirements, competitive dynamics, and field support requirements | |
| 25 | | Sanctioned Countries/ Customers | Clearly defined and documented due diligence process for proactively identifying potential matches against OFAC's Specifically Designated Nationals list for new (and existing) customers | |

APPENDIX B:

# Summary of Helpful Planning Resources

Please see www.terrafirmastrategy.com/resources/terralinks for hyperlinks

| | |
|---|---|
| Deloitte Tax Guides | Detailed tax information by country |
| WorldTariff | International customs, duty and tax info |
| World Business Culture | By country reports on various issues |
| AGOA Trade Profiles | African profiles and trade info |
| By Country Import/Export Information | By country import resources |
| Trade Services Directory | Database of 150,000 service providers |
| UN ComTrade | Detailed global trade data |
| FDI Stats | FDI and other economic stats for 200 economies |
| Global Industry Analyses | Market analyses by industry and country |
| Country/Indicator Trade Data | Trading Economics site searchable database |
| Investment Country Profiles | UN investment country profiles |
| Trade Policy Reviews | WTO resource searchable by country |
| WTO Trade Stats | Annual report, includes trade maps |
| Eurostat | Broad database of EU stats |
| Comparator | Tool to compare countries across economic indicators |

# SUMMARY OF HELPFUL PLANNING RESOURCES | 163

| | |
|---|---|
| Country Commercial Guides | Country reports prepared by US embassies |
| World Fact Book | Detailed information on 267 world entities |
| ADB Statistics | Economic and poverty statistics for Asia |
| WITS Trade/Tariffs | Great snapshot, some info requires subscription |
| WB Doing Business Indicators | Measures ease of doing business by country |
| Statista | Pay per report; huge statistical database |
| BBC Country Profiles | Profiles of countries and territories |
| Interactive Rankings | Rank countries by dozens of indicators |
| Monthly Bulletin of Stats | UN searchable database |
| International Data Base | US Census Bureau international statistics |
| WB Investing Across Borders | World Bank indicators of FDI regulation |
| Viewswire | Customizable news on 200 economies |
| International Labor Comparisons | Int'l labor comparisons for major industrial countries |
| Comparative (Legal) Guides | Cross border legal research tool |
| Law Firms by Region | Chambers rankings of legal resources |
| EFIC Country Profiles | Profiles on risks of doing business in different countries |

Made in the USA
Monee, IL
26 July 2021